The Freshwater Angler™

TROUT

THE COMPLETE GUIDE

to Catching Trout with Flies, Artificial Lures and Live Bait

NO LONGER PROPERTY OF
DENVER PUBLIC LIBRARY

The Freshwater Angler™

TROUT

THE COMPLETE GUIDE
to Catching Trout with Flies, Artificial Lures and Live Bait

John van Vliet

Creative Publishing international

Minneapolis, Minnesota

John van Vliet is the author of more than half a dozen books on fly fishing and fly tying, including the best-selling *The Art of Fly Tying*. An avid trout fisherman and fly tier, he has fly fished throughout the world and is a regular contributor to the *New York Times*.

Creative Publishing international

Copyright © 2008
Creative Publishing international, Inc.,
an imprint of Quarto Publishing
Group USA Inc., 400 First Avenue
North, Suite 400
Minneapolis, MN 55401
1-800-328-3895
www.creativepub.com

All rights reserved

President/CEO: Ken Fund
VP for Sales & Marketing: Kevin Hamric
Publisher: Bryan Trandem
Acquisitions Editor: Barbara Harold
Production Managers: Laura Hokkanen, Linda Halls

Creative Director: Michele Lanci-Altomare
Senior Design Managers: Brad Springer, Jon Simpson
Design Managers: Sara Holle, James Kegley
Book Design & Cover Design: Emily Brackett
Page Layout: Emily Brackett, DeAnne McCaslin
Illustrators: Maynard Reece, Jon Q. Wright
Principal Photographer: William Lindner
Contributing Photographers: Joel Arrington; Frank
  Balthis; Hiliary Bates; Erwin and Peggy Bauer;
  Barry Beck; Randy Binder/Minnesota Department
  of Natural Resources; Joseph Cella; Bob and Clara
  Calhoun/Bruce Coleman, Inc.; Mark Emery; Ted
  Fauceglia; Bob Firth; Jeff Foott; David H. Funk; Calvin
  Gates; John Goplin; Daniel Halsey; Tracy Holte; Paul
  Horsted/South Dakota Tourism; David L. Hughes;
  Spike Knuth/Virginia Department of Game and
  Inland Fisheries; Mark Macemon; Mark Miller; Al
  Noraker, Wright & McGill Co., Fly Girl Brand; Jack
  Olson/Colorado DNR; The Orvis Company, Inc.;
  C. Boyd Pfeiffer; Buzz Ramsey; Lynn Rogers; Mark
  Romanack; Stephen Ross, William Roston; Ron Schara;
  Dick Sternberg; Ben Streitz; University of Washington
  Fisheries Institute; Jeffrey Vanuga/OVIS; Yukio Yamada

Researchers: Robert Merila, Ben Streitz, Mike Hehner,
  Jim Moynagh, Eric Lindberg

Library of Congress Cataloging-in-Publication Data
Van Vliet, John.
  Trout : the complete guide / John van Vliet.
    p. cm. -- (Freshwater angler)
Includes index.
  ISBN-13: 978-01-58923-372-0 (hard cover)
  ISBN-10: 1-58923-372-7 (hard cover)
  1. Trout fishing--United States. 2. Salmon fishing--
United States.
I. Title. II. Series.

SH688.U6V37 2008
799.1'757--dc22

2007033544

This edition ISBN - 13: 978-1-59186-631-2

All photographs © Creative Publishing except:
  © Barry Beck: pg. 70
  © Bill Lindner: pgs. 76, 100
  © Wright & McGill: pg. 63 (top right)
  © C. Boyd Pfeiffer: pg. 128

All rights reserved. No part of this work covered by
the copyrights hereon may be reproduced or used in
any form or by any means—graphic, electronic, or
mechanical, including photocopying, recording, taping
of information on storage and retrieval systems—
without the written permission of the publisher.

CONTENTS

Introduction...6

Chapter 1: Trout and Salmon Basics...................................8

Stream Dwelling Trout and Salmon 11
Senses.................................... 15
Feeding and Growth...................... 18
Spawning Behavior 25
Hatchery Trout vs. Wild Trout 28
Habitat 29
Understanding Moving Water 38
Weather 42

Chapter 2: Equipment...44

Fly Rods and Reels 46
Fly Line................................. 50
Fly Leaders 54
Spinning and Baitcasting Tackle.......... 57
Trout-Fishing Accessories 59

Chapter 3: Stream Fishing Basics 64

Wading.................................. 66
Hooking, Playing and Landing Trout 67
Catch-and-Release 70
Fishing for Trophy Trout................. 72

Chapter 4: Fly Fishing for Trout and Salmon 74

Rigging Up 77
Casting a Fly............................ 79
Fishing with Dry Flies.................... 84
Fishing with Wet Flies 87
Fishing with Nymphs.................... 89
Fishing with Streamers 92
Fishing with Special-Purpose Flies 94

Chapter 5: Spinning and Baitcasting Techniques...................96

Jig Fishing............................... 98
Casting with Hardware.................. 100
Trolling................................. 103
Spinfishing with Flies 105
Natural Bait 107
Drift Fishing........................... 109
Plunking............................... 111

Chapter 6: Techniques for Special Situations 112

High Water.............................. 114
Low Water 115
Heavy Cover 116
Night Fishing 118
Winter Fishing 120

Chapter 7: Blue-Ribbon Trout Streams............................122

Eastern Streams 124
Midwestern Streams.................... 126
Southern Streams...................... 128
Western Streams....................... 130
Canadian Streams...................... 132
Great Lakes Tributaries................. 134
Coastal Streams 136

A few Words on Conservation 138

Index 140

INTRODUCTION

Trout have always held a special place in the hearts of anglers. Perhaps it is because of the beauty of the fish themselves, or of the places where trout live. Whatever the reason, trout are a popular gamefish with anglers of all ages and skill levels. But trout have a reputation of being "intelligent" and tough to catch. So, what does it take to become an accomplished trout angler?

In stream-trout fishing, versatility is the key to success. Trout streams undergo dramatic changes over the course of the year, and no single technique can be expected to work all the time.

In spring, when heavy rains and snowmelt cause streams to run high and muddy, fly fishing is tough. But you can still catch trout by spinfishing with small plugs, spinners, and spoons. If the water is exceptionally muddy, live bait (if permitted) may be the only answer. When the streams subside and the water clears, trout feed heavily on insects and fly fishing yields the best results.

Regardless of whether your interests lie more in fly fishing or in spinning, this book will show you how to catch stream trout under a wide range of conditions. We start by helping you understand trout behavior. You'll learn how trout detect danger, find food, select cover, and react to changes in weather.

Then, we'll give you a concise course on selecting stream-fishing equipment, including fly rods, lines and leaders, spinning and baitcasting tackle. We'll show you how to stock your fishing vest and how to choose a good pair of waders.

The fly-fishing section starts with complete instructions for rigging your tackle properly, something that too many beginning fly fisherman don't do. Every important fly-fishing tactic is presented using a no-nonsense approach. The basic fly-casting techniques are demonstrated with clear photos that make each step easy to understand, even for a beginner. You'll learn the most productive ways to fish dry flies, wet flies, nymphs, streamers, and special-purpose flies.

The spinning and baitcasting section details everything from the basic casting, trolling and drift-fishing techniques, as well as jigging, freelining, and plunking. And we'll even show you how to use flies with spinning tackle. After you learn all the best ways to catch trout, we'll give you instructions on the right way to release them so you can do your part to ensure quality fishing in years to come.

A section on special situations will help you catch trout under conditions that cause big problems for many stream-trout anglers. You'll learn the tricks that help experts catch lots of trout in high water or low water, in heavy cover, at night, and even in winter. We'll also reveal the secrets of catching trophy trout.

Completing the book is a roundup of the top North American trout regions, including the types of rivers and the species you'll find in them.

Whether you're an experienced angler or you're completely new to fishing, this book will help you catch more trout.

Chapter 1

TROUT AND SALMON BASICS

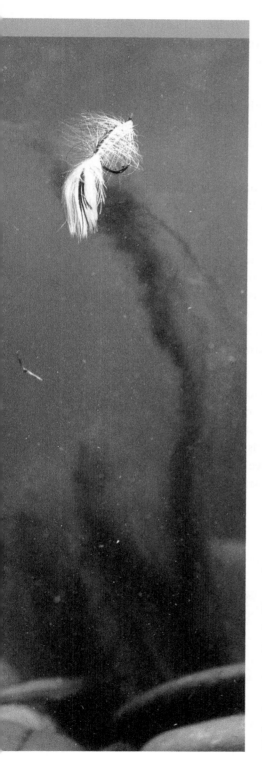

Trout and salmon have long been considered superior gamefish, the ultimate in wariness and fighting ability. In years past, many anglers regarded them as the only true gamefish.

Unfortunately, this wary nature has led to the popular notion that the fish are intelligent, and therefore difficult for the average angler to catch. However, there is no evidence to indicate they are more intelligent than other gamefish species.

The notion of intelligence is reinforced when anglers see feeding trout being "put down" by even the slightest movement or vibration. However, this is an instinctive reaction, and should not be confused with intelligence. Like any other fish, trout flee for cover to avoid predators. As soon as they hatch, trout face attacks from predatory insects, crayfish, and other small fish. As they grow older, trout are attacked by larger fish and by kingfishers, herons, and other predatory birds. A trout's wariness is also the result of natural selection; those that lack sufficient wariness do not live to reproduce.

Their preference for cold water distinguishes trout and salmon from other gamefish. Although temperature preferences vary among trout and salmon species, most seek water temperatures from 50 to 65°F (10 to 18°C), and avoid temperatures above 70°F (21°C). This requirement means they can live only in streams or lakes fed by cold water sources such as springs or snowmelt, or in lakes with deep, unpolluted water.

Trout and salmon belong to the family Salmonidae. Besides trout and salmon, the family includes grayling, found mainly in Alaska, the Yukon, and the Northwest Territories; and whitefish, which are widely distributed in the northern states and Canada but have minor importance to anglers.

For the purposes of this book, the term "trout" includes not only true trout (genus *Oncorhynchus* and *Salmo*) but also chars (genus *Salvelinus*). True trout, such as browns and rainbows, have dark spots on a light background; chars, such as brook trout and Dolly Varden, have light spots on a dark background. Chars require colder water than true trout.

Dark spots on light background: Trout and Atlantic Salmon

Light spots on dark background: Char

Atlantic salmon are closely related to brown trout and belong to the same genus, *Salmo*. Pacific salmon belong to a different genus, *Oncorhynchus*, meaning "hooknose," and are related to rainbow trout. Pacific salmon spawn only once, dying soon afterward; other members of the family may live to spawn several times. All salmon species are anadromous; they spend their lives at sea, and then return to freshwater streams to spawn. Salmon stocked in freshwater lakes spawn in lake tributaries.

Many species of trout, including rainbow, brook, brown, and cutthroat, have anadromous forms with a different appearance than the forms limited to freshwater. The anadromous forms are generally sleeker and more silvery.

Powerful fighters, trout and salmon have remarkable stamina. Some species, like rainbow trout and Atlantic salmon, leap repeatedly when hooked; others, like brook trout, wage a deep, bulldog-style battle. Most trout and salmon are excellent eating, but there is a strong trend toward catch-and-release fishing. In some heavily fished water, catch-and-release is mandatory. This has long been the accepted practice for Atlantic salmon because the species is so rare and so treasured as a gamefish. Catch-and-release fishing ensures that the fish remain in a stream long enough to spawn and produce "wild" progeny. The other alternative, frowned upon by most trout enthusiasts, is put-and-take stocking of hatchery-reared trout.

To become a successful trout or salmon angler, you must shed the notion that there is an aura of mystery surrounding these fish. Although they live in prettier settings than most other fish, they have the same behavior patterns and the same needs for food and cover. Learn to think of their basic needs and you will have no trouble finding them. Learn to approach them stealthily, like a predator, and you will have no trouble catching them.

Dorsal Fin

Adipose Fin

Caudal Fin

Gill Cover

Pectoral Fin

Pelvic Fin

Anal Fin

STREAM DWELLING TROUT AND SALMON

Practically all North American species of trout and salmon can be found in streams at some time of the year. Even lake dwelling trout swim into streams in spring or fall to spawn. Only the lake trout (*Salvelinus namaycush*), a species not covered in this book, spawns primarily in lakes. Following are brief descriptions of the trout and salmon species that stream fishermen are most likely to encounter.

TROUT AND ATLANTIC SALMON

RAINBOW TROUT
Oncorhynchus mykiss

All rainbows have radiating rows of black spots on tail, black spots on back and sides, and no teeth or tongue. Common rainbows have a pinkish horizontal band and pinkish gill cover with some black spots. May grow to exceed 25 pounds (11.3 kg).

COASTAL RAINBOW TROUT (STEELHEAD)
Oncorhynchus mykiss

Body longer and sleeker than that of common rainbow; fewer spots below lateral line. Steelhead may have pale pinkish horizontal band and gill cover, but gill cover has few or no black spots. May grow to more than 40 pounds (18.1 kg).

BROWN TROUT
Salmo trutta

Square tail with few or no spots; adipose fin (arrow) with some spots. Sides light brownish to yellowish with black spots and usually some red or orange spots. Spots often have whitish to bluish halos. May grow to more than 40 pounds (18.1 kg).

YELLOWSTONE CUTTHROAT TROUT
Oncorhynchus clarki bouvieri

All cutthroat have reddish slash marks on throat, black spots on tail, and patch of teeth at base of tongue. Yellowstones have spots above and below lateral line; spots are more concentrated toward rear.

COASTAL CUTTHROAT TROUT
Oncorhynchus clarki clarki

Sides and back heavily spotted; spots uniformly distributed from front to rear. Background color more silvery than that of other subspecies of cutthroat, and reddish slash marks on throat may be faint.

WEST SLOPE CUTTHROAT TROUT
Oncorhynchus clarki lewisi

Spots on West Slope cutthroat are even more concentrated toward rear than those on Yellowstone cutthroat. But the spots are somewhat smaller, and usually absent on front half of body below lateral line.

GOLDEN TROUT
Oncorhynchus mykiss aguabonita

Golden sides with reddish horizontal band that runs through about 10 dusky, oval-shaped marks. Tail spotted. Dorsal, pelvic, and anal fins with white tips. May grow to exceed 10 pounds (4.5 kg).

ATLANTIC SALMON
Salmo salar

Sides silvery to yellowish brown. Like brown trout, Atlantic salmon have few or no spots on tail. Tail slightly forked rather than square. Adipose fin unspotted; adipose of brown spotted. May grow to more than 75 pounds (34 kg).

ARTIC GRAYLING
Thymallus arcticus

Dorsal fin with base at least as long as fish's head; fin has rows of blue or violet spots. Pelvic fins with light streaks. Sides violet-gray and silver with small dark spots. May grow to exceed 5 pounds (2.3 kg).

CHARS

BROOK TROUT (SPECKLED TROUT)
Salvelinus fontinalis

Background color brownish to greenish. Back laced with light, wormlike marks; sides have light spots and some red spots, both with blue halos. Lower fins with white leading edges. May grow to more than 12 pounds (5.4 kg).

ARCTIC CHAR
Salvelinus alpinus

Background color silvery green. Sides with pinkish, reddish, or cream-colored spots, some at least as large as pupil of eye. Lower fins with white leading edges. May grow to more than 30 pounds (13.6 kg).

BULL TROUT
Salvelinus confluentus

Sides silvery green to dark green with pinkish to whitish spots. Lower fins with white leading edges. Head considerably longer, broader, and more flattened than that of Dolly Varden. May grow to exceed 30 pounds (13.6 kg).

DOLLY VARDEN
Salvelinus malma

Silvery green sides with pinkish, reddish, or whitish spots. Lower fins with white leading edges. Resembles Arctic char and bull trout, but spots smaller than char's, and head less flattened than bull's. May grow to more than 10 pounds (4.5 kg).

CHINOOK SALMON (KING SALMON)
Oncorhynchus tshawytscha

Sides silvery; upper sides, back, and both lobes of tail peppered with small black spots. Teeth set in blackish gums. Anal fin, usually with 15 to 19 rays, is longer than that of other Pacific salmon. May grow to nearly 100 pounds (45.4 kg).

COHO SALMON (SILVER SALMON)
Oncorhynchus kisutch

Resembles chinook, but tail with small black spots on upper lobe only. Teeth set in whitish to grayish gums. Anal fin considerably shorter than that of chinook, usually with 12 to 15 rays. May grow to more than 30 pounds (13.6 kg).

PINK SALMON (HUMPBACK SALMON)
Oncorhynchus gorbuscha

Sides silvery; upper sides, back, and entire tail with large black spots, some as large as eye. Spots on back, sides, and tail of chinook much smaller than eye. May grow to exceed 10 pounds (4.5 kg).

SOCKEYE SALMON (RED SALMON)
Oncorhynchus nerka

Silvery sides with brilliant bluish to greenish back, often with black speckles. Tail unspotted. Resembles chum salmon, but lacks the faint vertical bands. May grow to exceed 10 pounds (4.5 kg).

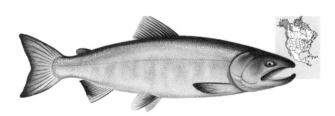

CHUM SALMON (DOG SALMON)
Oncorhynchus keta

Sides silvery, often with black speckles on the back but no distinct black spots. Faint vertical bands on the side intensify as spawning time nears. Tail unspotted. May grow to exceed 30 pounds (13.6 kg).

SENSES

Stream fishermen know that a sudden movement, a heavy footstep, a shadow, or a fly rod glinting in sunlight will send a trout scurrying for cover. Salmonids depend mainly on vision to detect danger, but they also have an excellent sense of smell and a well-developed lateral-line sense.

VISION. When approaching salmonids, remember that they can view the outside world clearly through a "window," a circular area on the surface of the water whose size depends on the depth of the fish. The diameter is slightly more than twice as wide as the fish is deep. A trout at a depth of 2 feet (0.61 m) would have a window 4 feet, 6 inches (1.2 m, 15.2 cm) wide. Surrounding the window, the surface is a mirror, so the fish can't see out.

Many frustrated fishermen can attest that salmonids have excellent color vision. An olive nymph may produce fish after fish, but a similar nymph in a slightly darker green will not draw a strike. Because the

When approaching salmonids, remember that they can view the outside world clearly through a "window," a circular area on the surface of the water whose size depends on the depth of the fish. The diameter is slightly more than twice as wide as the fish is deep. A trout at a depth of 2 feet (60 cm) would have a window 4 feet, 6 inches (1.4 m) wide. Surrounding the window, the surface is a mirror, so the fish can't see out.

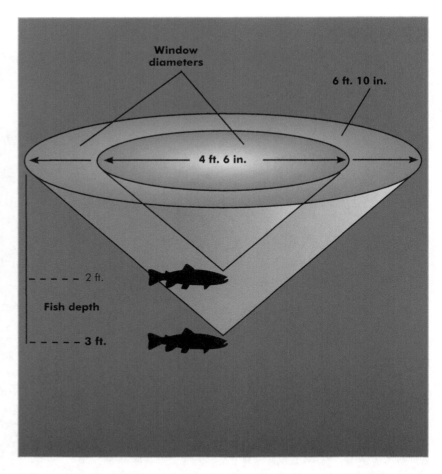

Window diameters

6 ft. 10 in.

4 ft. 6 in.

2 ft.

Fish depth

3 ft.

fish are so color selective, experienced anglers often carry similar fly or lure patterns in several different colors or shades in an attempt to determine the color of the day.

Trout and salmon have only fair night vision. With the exception of large brown trout, they do little feeding after dark. Even browns seem to have difficulty locating a fly unless it produces noise or vibration.

SMELL. Trout and salmon use their sense of smell to find food, avoid predators, and locate spawning areas. If you drop a gob of fresh salmon eggs in a clear pond filled with rainbows, the eggs will "milk" as they sink, leaving a scent trail. Feeding trout mill about until they cross the trail, then they turn and follow it to the eggs.

Researchers in British Columbia found that salmon turned back from their spawning run and headed downstream when a bear was fishing upstream of them. The salmon detected a chemical emitted by the bear called L-serine. This chemical is also given off by human skin.

Salmon and migratory forms of trout navigate at sea or in large lakes by using the sun, currents, and the earth's magnetic field. These clues enable them to return to the vicinity of their home stream at spawning

Salmon returning to spawn use their keen sense of smell to detect the presence of bears far upstream.

time. Once they get that far, they rely on scent to find just the right stream. Amazingly, they can return to the exact area of the stream where their lives began. When researchers cut a salmon's olfactory nerves, it could not find its way back.

Biologists have discovered that they can dramatically increase the percentage of chinook salmon returning to a given stream by "imprinting" the young fish before they move to open water. Just as the young start to smolt, a chemical that can be detected in extremely low concentrations is dripped into the stream. The smell of this chemical is somehow locked into the fish's memory. Then, when the salmon reach maturity, the same chemical is again dripped into the stream. In some cases, this technique has doubled the return rate.

LATERAL LINE. Veteran stream fishermen step very lightly when wading the streambed or walking the bank, even when outside the fish's field of vision. They also realize that vibration-producing lures work better in murky water or after dark than lures that produce little vibration. The fish evidently detect footsteps and lure vibrations with their lateral-line system, a network of ultra-sensitive nerve endings along the side of the body.

FEEDING AND GROWTH

During their early years, trout and salmon feed mainly on immature forms of aquatic insects, and to a lesser extent on adult insects, both aquatic and terrestrial. They also eat small crustaceans, mollusks, and earthworms. As they grow larger, they continue to eat large numbers of insects, but small fish make up an increasing percentage of their diet. Large trout do not hesitate to eat small animals like frogs and mice. Some salmon species, such as sockeye and pink, are plankton feeders, filtering tiny organisms from the water with their closely spaced gill rakers. This feeding behavior makes them very difficult to catch on hook and line. Practically all trout and salmon will eat the eggs and young of other species, and of their own kind, when the opportunity presents itself.

How fast a trout grows depends not only on the type of food it eats, but also on the fertility and size of the stream.

Generally, trout that feed primarily on insects grow more slowly than those that eat small fish; insect feeding uses more energy for nutrients obtained. Trout in mountain streams usually grow slower than trout in farm-country streams. The high altitude streams are colder and less fertile, so they produce considerably less food. Brown trout, for instance, seldom exceed 1 pound (0.45 kg) in small mountain streams where insects are the major food. In contrast, they grow to 15 pounds (7.4 kg) or more in rivers with marginal temperatures for trout but with plenty of baitfish.

Trout that live in small brooks have a slower growth rate than those in good-sized rivers because the bigger water offers a greater abundance and diversity of foods. The size of the spawning stream also seems to affect the size of chinook salmon, even though the salmon do very little feeding in the stream. Studies have revealed that the larger the spawning stream, the larger the salmon.

Genetics also influence growth rate. Fast-growing strains of many species have evolved naturally or have been produced by fish culturists who select and breed the fastest-growing individuals from each year-class. Donaldson rainbow trout, a strain selectively bred for fast growth at the University of Washington, may reach 10 pounds (4.5 kg) in only two years, provided they have enough food. A normal rainbow of the same age weighs less than a pound (0.45 kg), even if food is abundant.

Male trout and salmon grow faster than females; salmonids differ in this respect from most other fish species.

SALMONID DIET AND LIFE SPAN		
Species	Common Foods	Max. Age
Rainbow trout	Mainly insects; also plankton, fish eggs, small fish, crustaceans	11
Brown trout	Primarily insects; large browns feed mostly on fish and crayfish	8
Cutthroat trout	Mostly insects and small fish; also fish eggs, crustaceans, and frogs	9
Golden trout	Insects, especially caddisfly and midge larvae; also crustaceans	7
Brook trout	Mainly insects and small fish; diet extremely varied	15
Bull trout	Mainly fish; also insects, mollusks, and crustaceans	19
Dolly Varden	Mainly small fish and fish eggs; also insects	19
Arctic char	Small fish, fish eggs, insects, and plankton	40
Arctic grayling	Mainly insects and fish eggs; also small fish, mollusks, and crustaceans	10
Pink salmon	Plankton, crustaceans, squid, and small fish	Normally 2, up to 3
Chinook salmon	Mostly fish; also shrimps, squid, and crustaceans	Normally 4, up to 9
Coho salmon	Mainly fish; also crustaceans	Normally 3, up to 5
Chum salmon	Plankton, small fish, squid, and crustaceans	Normally 4, up to 7
Sockeye salmon	Mostly plankton and small crustaceans; also small fish and bottom organisms	Normally 4, up to 8
Atlantic salmon	Crustaceans, insects, and small fish	14

Common Stream Insects

In the quest to "match the hatch," some fly-fishing enthusiasts spend many hours studying stream insects and tying flies that closely mimic the real thing. Some experts can identify hundreds of different insect species and tie flies to match. However, in most situations, you do not have to duplicate hatching insects so precisely. If you can recognize the insect group, and the life stage of the group that the trout are feeding on, and then use a fly about the same size, shape, and color, you can catch all but the most selective trout.

Stream insects are grouped into four major orders represented by thousands of species. These orders include mayflies, caddisflies, stoneflies, and midges.

MAYFLIES. Among the most common aquatic insects in eastern and midwestern streams, mayflies are especially abundant in limestone streams and spring creeks. They normally have a one-year life span, most of which they spend as a nymph. Mayfly nymphs are easily recognized by the single pair of wing pads, and gills on the upper surface of the abdomen. Most species have three long tail filaments.

When a mayfly nymph matures, it swims to the surface, its skin splits down the back, and a subimago, or dun, emerges. The dun drifts on the surface until its wings dry, and during this time it is an easy target for trout. It then flies to streamside vegetation and after a day or two transforms into a sexually mature adult, or spinner. Duns have grayish or brownish upright wings; spinners have clear upright wings, more vibrant colors, and longer tail filaments. Mayflies are the only aquatic insects with this two-step adult stage.

STAGES OF A MAYFLY

Mayfly nymph (left); mayfly subimago, or dun (middle); mayfly adult, or spinner (right).

STONEFLIES. These insects abound in the West, especially in cold mountain streams. They will not tolerate pollution or warm water, so they make good indicators of water quality.

Like a mayfly, a stonefly spends most of its aquatic life as a nymph. The nymphal stage lasts from one to four years. Stonefly nymphs have two pairs of wing pads instead of one, two short tail filaments instead of three long ones, and the gills are on the underside of the thorax, rather than the upper surface of the abdomen. Adults are dull-colored, with wings that lie flat against the back.

CADDISFLIES. In the majority of trout streams, caddisflies are the most common aquatic insect. They are more tolerant of pollution and warm water than most other aquatic insects. Their life cycle consists of two aquatic stages, the larva and the pupa. The small wormlike larva is cream-colored, with a dark head and three sets of jointed legs near the front of the body. It often lives in a case built from sand grains, twigs, or other debris. The larval cases are commonly attached to rocks. Some larvae roam freely over the bottom, with or without cases. These are the ones most often eaten by trout.

After about a year, the larvae seal themselves into their cases to pupate. These cases are usually attached to a rock or other object. Inside the cases, the pupae develop legs and wing pads. After a few weeks they chew through their cases, crawl out, and dart for the surface. There, they transform quickly into adults and fly away. The adults are grayish or brownish, with tent-like wings.

Overall, caddis larvae are much more important as trout food than the pupae or adults. Although trout will eat pupae in their cases, the pupae are most vulnerable as they swim for the surface.

STAGES OF A CADDISFLY

Caddisly larva with case (left); caddisfly adult (right).

Midge larvae (left); midge adult (right).

MIDGES. This group includes the tiniest aquatic insects. Midges are most numerous in slow-moving, vegetated stream stretches. Like caddisflies, midges have larval and pupal stages.

Midge larvae are more slender than caddis larvae. They do not have jointed legs or live in cases. Normally, the larvae cling to vegetation or bottom debris. Some burrow into mucky bottoms. A trout may consume hundreds of the tiny larvae each day.

After several months the larvae begin to pupate, but some kinds do not form cases to do this. Instead, they move about actively for about two weeks before maturing and swimming to the surface. The legs of adult midges are long, especially the forelegs, and look quite frail. Trout feed heavily on the pupal and adult forms.

One sure way to find out what a trout has been eating is to pump its stomach. But first you have to catch a trout. Even with no trout in hand, you can get an idea of their diet by seining with a fine-mesh net or turning over rocks, then examining the clinging insects.

A hatch chart can give you some guidelines on the type of insect likely to be hatching in your region at a certain time of year and time of day. But hatch charts can be misleading, because different streams in the same region have different hatches, and hatching times can vary by several weeks depending on the weather.

You may be able to get more specific information on hatches in a particular stream by inquiring at a local fly shop.

Understanding the Rise

A rise is the surface disturbance that results when a trout or salmon takes a floating insect. A rise can tell you not only where the fish is located, but also what it is eating. Inexperienced anglers often make the mistake of casting directly to a rise in hopes of catching the trout. However, in most cases, the rise occurs well downstream of the trout's lie. To present your fly where the trout is holding, you must cast well upstream of the rise. By watching exactly how trout are rising, you can get an idea of what type of insect they are taking. You may be able to determine the life stage of the insect, the group it belongs to, and possibly the exact species. This information helps you arrive at a strategy for catching the trout.

HOW A TROUT TAKES A FLOATING INSECT

Feeding trout face into the current. They watch the surface closely to spot insects or other food drifting into their window of vision.

After spotting an insect, a trout drifts downstream tail first while carefully examining the food. The trout may drift only a foot or two (30 to 60 cm), or as much as 25 feet (7.6 m).

The trout rises to take the insect, leaving a noticeable ring on the surface. The tendency of most anglers is to cast just upstream of the ring.

Immediately after rising, the trout returns upstream to its lie. If you cast just above the ring, your fly alights too far downstream, behind the trout's window of vision.

SIP RISE. Generally means trout are surface-feeding on mayfly duns or stoneflies. A trout sucks in the insect without breaking the surface. In smooth water you see a wing; in broken water it may not be apparent. Cast a dry mayfly or stonefly imitation well ahead of the rise.

HEAD-AND-TAIL RISE. Usually means the trout is feeding on insects in the surface film. The head appears first; then, as the fish rolls, you see the dorsal fin, and finally the tail. Cast a spinner, terrestrial, nymph, or midge pupa well upstream of the rise and let it drift naturally.

SPLASH. The trout completely clears the water, usually to catch emerging insects such as caddisflies, or insects dipping in the water to deposit eggs. Use a wet fly, angle your cast downstream, then let the current swing the fly to the trout. Or, skate a caddis dry fly on the surface.

TAILING. Technically, this is not a rise because the fish is not feeding on the surface. When you see a protruding tail, the trout is probably rooting immature insects or scuds from the bottom. Drift a nymph or scud pattern along the bottom to the fish.

SPAWNING BEHAVIOR

Salmonid spawning habits vary greatly among species. Most spawn in fall, but some, like the rainbow trout, spawn in spring. Trout, char, grayling, and Atlantic salmon can live to spawn several times. Salmonids require flowing water to spawn, but brook trout and sockeye salmon sometimes spawn in lakes. All but the grayling dig a redd, or nest, for depositing their eggs.

PHYSICAL CHANGES. Before spawning, trout and salmon, particularly the males, undergo astounding anatomical changes. A male's jaws lengthen and the lower jaw develops a large hook, or kype. The teeth of male Pacific salmon grow much larger before spawning, evidently to help them defend their territories. Male pinks and sockeyes develop a pronounced hump on the back, just ahead of the dorsal fin. Their grotesque appearance may also intimidate predators and competing males that approach the spawning site.

Both sexes undergo dramatic color changes. Color shifts are different for the different species, but in most cases the colors become considerably darker and more intense. The most pronounced are in Pacific salmon. As spawning time approaches and their bodies begin to deteriorate, they change from bright silver to brilliant red, olive green, or even black.

SPAWNING SITE. Trout and salmon prefer a clean gravel bottom for spawning, usually at the tail of a pool or in some other area where the current sweeps the bottom free of silt.

The female digs the redd. She turns on her side and beats her tail against the bottom, moving the gravel away and creating a depression longer than her body and about half as deep.

As the female digs, she is often accompanied by more than one male; the largest male is dominant and defends his territory by charging the smaller ones, using his kype to nip them. A female commonly digs several redds, depositing a portion of her eggs in each.

SPAWNING ACT. The dominant male courts the female by nudging and quivering. Finally, the two lay side by side in the redd. They become rigid, arch their backs, and with their mouths agape, vibrate to release sperm and eggs. Sometimes, the other males also deposit sperm in the redd.

After spawning, the female digs at the upstream edge of the redd, covering the eggs with several inches of gravel. When all spawning activity is completed, the parents abandon the redd. Female Pacific salmon try to guard their redds for a short time, but they soon weaken and die. Salmonids do not attempt to guard their young after they hatch.

Male brook trout undergo a dramatic color change during spawning, changing from their normal coloration (top) to vividly pronounced colors (bottom).

Male Pacific salmon undergo astounding physical changes just prior to spawning.

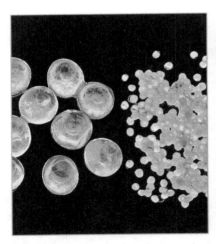

Salmon and trout produce fewer and larger eggs than most other freshwater gamefish. Salmon eggs (left) are much larger than walleye eggs (right).

All species of trout and salmon, except the golden trout, lose their parr marks as they mature.

EGGS AND INCUBATION. Trout and salmon are less prolific than most other gamefish. They have very large eggs, few in number. A 10-pound (4.5 kg) rainbow deposits only about 4,000 eggs; a walleye of the same size, for comparison, deposits about 200,000.

Salmonid eggs incubate from one to five months, depending on species. This long incubation period subjects the eggs to many hazards, such as disease and flooding. Predators such as crayfish, insects, and other fish, including trout, quickly eat eggs that are not well buried.

JUVENILE STAGES. The eggs hatch in the gravel, and at first the fry can move very little. They do not feed, but get nutrients from the attached yolk sac. After several weeks, they gain enough strength to wiggle through the gravel and emerge into the stream. Soon afterward, the fry absorb the yolk sac and begin feeding on plankton.

As the fish grow, they develop a row of dark, oval-shaped marks along the side. At this stage the fish are called parr; the markings are called parr marks.

In the case of anadromous fish like salmon and steelhead, the young spend at least six months, and sometimes as long as three years, in the home stream before they start to develop migratory tendencies. As the migratory urge develops, the parr marks start to disappear, the sides turn a brilliant silver, and the fish begin moving downstream. This process is called smolting, and the young at this stage are called smolts. The smolts spend several years at sea or in a large lake before reaching maturity.

Predation is severe during a trout's early life. Kingfishers, herons, otters, and fish take the greatest toll. As a rule, less than 1 percent of newly hatched fry survive to age one.

HOMING. Salmon are known for their uncanny ability to return to their home stream to spawn, swimming thousands of miles (km) across oceans and up rivers. Trout have the same ability to a lesser extent.

Although migratory salmonids sometimes stray to other rivers, the vast majority return to the same river, and usually to the precise area of that river, where they hatched years earlier.

Where spawning streams have been polluted or blocked by dams, salmon populations decline or disappear because the fish do not seek out alternative streams.

WHEN SALMONIDS SPAWN	
Species	**Time of Year**
Rainbow trout	Spring
Brown trout	Fall
Cutthroat trout	Spring
Golden trout	Midsummer
Brook trout	Early fall
Bull trout	Early fall
Dolly Varden	Fall
Arctic char	Fall
Arctic grayling	Early spring
Pink salmon	Fall
Chinook salmon	Fall
Coho salmon	Late fall
Chum salmon	Fall
Sockeye salmon	Fall
Atlantic salmon	Fall

HATCHERY TROUT VS. WILD TROUT

Hatchery trout (bottom) are easily distinguished from wild trout (top). They lack the brilliant coloration of wild trout, and in many cases their fins are worn from constant rubbing against the hatchery's concrete raceways.

To many trout enthusiasts, "hatchery trout" are dirty words. Whirling disease and other fish-killing viruses were originally linked to hatchery-reared fish. However, trout fishermen also realize that without hatchery-reared trout they would have fewer trout fishing opportunities.

There is no denying that hatchery-reared trout lack many of the desirable attributes of wild ones. They are much less wary and considerably easier for anglers and predators to catch. When hooked, they wage a comparatively weak battle and are much less likely to jump.

The main gripe against hatchery trout is that they compete for food and space with wild trout. Often, the size and number of trout in a stream increases dramatically when stocking is discontinued. Another problem is genetic contamination. When hatchery trout breed with wild ones, the offspring are less suited to the environment than the wild trout were.

Of course, hatcheries must stock streams that do not have suitable conditions for natural reproduction, if there is to be a trout fishery. Managers continue to stock catchable-size trout in many such put-and-take streams, particularly near large cities. Even so, the put-and-take management is gradually giving way to a put-and-grow philosophy; the trout are stocked as fry or fingerlings, and then allowed to grow up in the stream. This type of stocking is considerably less expensive, and the trout that survive to catchable size bear a much closer resemblance to wild trout.

HABITAT

Mention the term "trout stream," and most people think of flowing water that is cold, clear, and unpolluted. This stereotype is accurate, but there are other requirements as well. The quantity and size of trout a stream produces depend on the following:

WATER FERTILITY. A stream's fertility, or level of dissolved minerals, affects the production of plankton, the fundamental link in the aquatic food chain. The level of dissolved minerals depends mainly on the water source. Limestone streams generally have a considerably higher mineral content than freestone streams.

A limestone stream is normally fed by an underground spring rich in calcium carbonate, an important nutrient, and flows over a streambed that supplies even more minerals. Limestone streams have more aquatic vegetation, produce more insects and crustaceans, and generally grow more and larger trout.

A freestone stream is fed by runoff or springs with a low mineral content. It typically flows over a streambed that contributes few nutrients to the water. But some freestone streams pick up extra nutrients from fertile tributaries, so they produce good-sized trout.

WATER TEMPERATURE. All streams that support permanent trout populations have one thing in common: a reliable source of cold water.

The cold water often comes from springs or meltwater from snow or glaciers. Streams fed by ordinary surface runoff become too warm for trout in midsummer, except in the North or at high altitudes, where air temperatures stay cool all year.

Some trout can survive at surprisingly warm water temperatures. Browns and rainbows, for instance, live in streams where temperatures sometimes rise into the low 80s (27 to 29°C). Though at these temperatures they usually feed very little, their growth rate slows, and their resistance to disease diminishes.

The stream temperature depends not only on the water source, but also on the shape and gradient (slope) of the channel, and the amount of shade.

GRADIENT. The most productive trout streams have a relatively low gradient, from 0.5 to 2 percent, which converts to 25 to 100 feet (7.6 to 30.5 m) per mile (1.6 km). In other words, the streambed drops that

Silted or muddy streambeds produce few insects and are unsuitable for spawning.

Clean gravel or rubble streambeds are a good habitat for aquatic insects and provide the essential conditions required for spawning.

many feet for each mile of length. The higher the gradient, the faster the current flows.

Mountain streams may have a much higher gradient, sometimes as great as 15 percent. Above 7 percent, a stream must have stair-step pools, boulders, log jams, or other slack-water areas if it is to support trout.

A channel with a gradient less than 0.5 percent tends to have a silty bottom and water too warm for trout.

BOTTOM TYPE. A clean gravel or rubble bottom produces much more insect life than a sandy or silty bottom. It also makes a better spawning substrate.

Streambed siltation is a major problem facing many trout streams. Excess silt can result from logging, poor farming practices, and overgrazing of stream banks. The silt clogs up the spaces between the gravel, destroying insect habitat, and causing eggs deposited in the gravel to suffocate.

Conservation agencies often fence trout streams to keep out cattle, allowing vegetation to redevelop.

HABITAT DIVERSITY. A stream with diverse habitat generally produces more trout than one with uniform habitat throughout. Where the habitat is diverse, trout find a variety and abundance of food.

Many types of aquatic insects thrive in riffles and runs; baitfish and burrowing aquatic insects abound in pools. If a stream has aquatic vegetation like stonewort or watercress, the plants often host scuds, midge larvae, and other trout foods. Diverse habitat also provides plenty of resting and spawning areas.

Streams that meander in a snakelike pattern have greater habitat diversity than streams with a straight channel. Consequently, they have cover for trout that is more natural. As a stream winds along, banks along the outside bends become undercut and tree roots wash out, making ideal hiding spots.

Fisheries managers dread the prospect of stream channelization. They know that when the channel is artificially straightened, riffle-run-pool habitat disappears, and trout disappear with it.

SHAPE OF CHANNEL. A narrow, deep channel is generally better than a wide, shallow one. In the latter, a higher percentage of the water is exposed to the air and sun, causing the water to warm more rapidly.

Where the channel is too wide, there is not enough current to keep silt in suspension, so it settles out, smothering gravel beds that provide food and spawning habitat. Stream-improvement projects are often intended to narrow a channel that has been widened by eroding banks or beaver dams.

Meandering streams provide a diverse habitat for aquatic foods, critical cover, as well as resting and spawning areas.

Upper zone, or headwaters, normally has very cold water, a low flow, and a narrow streambed. The headwaters serve as a spawning and rearing area, but is too small to support large trout.

The middle zone has cool water and is the most productive part of the stream. It has the best insect populations and generally supports the highest population of adult trout.

The lower zone is generally warmer and the bottom may be silty or muddy. It supports the fewest trout, but may hold some of the largest ones, along with warmwater gamefish.

STABILITY OF FLOW. Almost any stream can support trout in spring, when water temperatures are cool and water flows are high. But trout must live in the stream year around. If the flow falls too low, even for a few days, trout will probably not survive.

Streams with a distinct cold water source commonly have temperature zones. The upper zone, or headwater, normally has very cold water, a low flow, and a narrow streambed. The headwater serves as a spawning and rearing area, but is too small to support large trout. Because of the cold water, it may hold brook trout. Along the stream course tributaries flow in, increasing the stream's size. The middle zone has cool water and is the most productive part of the stream. It has the best insect hatches and diversity, and generally supports the highest population of adult trout. As more tributaries flow in, the stream gets even larger and the streambed flattens out. The water is warm, the current is slow, and the bottom is silty. The lower zone supports few trout, but some of the largest ones. You may find big browns along with suckers, carp, and even catfish.

Low flows present the biggest problem in later summer, especially in areas with little forest cover to preserve ground moisture. If the weather is hot and there has been little rain, too much water evaporates from the stream, reducing the depth and slowing the current, so the remaining water warms faster. Even if trout survive the warm water, they are under so much stress that they do not feed. Low water can also be a problem in winter. In a dry year, winter flows may drop so low that the stream freezes to the bottom.

Large underground springs provide the most stability. They ensure at least a minimal flow so the stream doesn't dry up during a drought. And because spring water comes out of the ground at the same temperature year around, these streams stay cool in summer and relatively warm in winter.

SHADE. Most streams require some shade from trees or overhanging grasses to keep the water cool enough for trout. A stream that lacks sufficient shade will be cool enough in the upper reaches, but the water will warm rapidly as it moves downstream, so the trout zone is limited. A stream with too much shade may hold trout over most of its length, but the cold temperature inhibits food production and slows trout growth. Fisheries managers have found that they can maximize trout production by planting or removing trees to regulate the amount of shade.

WATER CLARITY. Most trout species prefer clear water, although some, like browns and rainbows, can tolerate low clarity. Clear water allows sunlight to penetrate to the streambed, promoting the growth of plants, which in turn produce trout food. Clear water also makes it easy for trout to see food and avoid predators, including anglers.

DISSOLVED OXYGEN. A lack of adequate dissolved oxygen is rarely a problem in trout streams, except in tailwater fisheries where cold, dense water from the depths of a reservoir must be aerated as it passes through the dam. In most streams, however, oxygen is replenished through contact with the air.

pH LEVEL. In most streams the exact pH level is of little importance to fishermen. Trout, like most fish, can tolerate a wide range of pH levels, and can live in waters with a pH as low as 4.5 or as high as 9.5. Nevertheless, extremely low pH levels resulting from acid rain have wiped out brook trout populations in parts of the Northeast. Many kinds of trout foods, like mayflies, are less tolerant of low pH levels than the trout themselves.

HABITAT PREFERENCES OF SALMONIDS	
Species	**Preferred Water Temp**
Rainbow trout	55-60°F (12.8–15.6°C)
Brown trout	60-65°F (15.6–18.3°C)
Cutthroat trout	55-62°F (12.9–16.7°C)
Golden trout	58-62°F (14.4–16.7°C)
Brook trout	52-56°F (11.1–13.3°C)
Bull trout	45-55°F (7.2–12.8°C)
Dolly Varden	50-55°F (10–12.8°C)
Arctic char	45-50°F (7.2–10°C)
Arctic grayling	42-50°F (5.6–10°C)
Pink salmon	52-57°F (11.1–13.9°C)
Chinook salmon	53-57°F (11.7–13.9°C)
Coho salmon	53-57°F (11.7–13.9°C)
Chum salmon	54-57°F (12.2–13.9°C)
Sockeye salmon	50-55°F (10–12.8°C)
Atlantic salmon	53-59°F (11.7–15°C)

Spring-fed tributaries cool the water below the point where they enter the stream. They attract trout in mid to late summer.

Undercut banks usually form along outside bends. They offer excellent midday cover, especially in sunny weather.

Riffles are morning and evening feeding areas. Trout and salmon usually spawn just above or below riffles, but may spawn right in them.

Runs, the deep, moderately fast moving areas between riffles and pools, hold trout almost anytime, if there is sufficient cover.

Pools are smoother and look darker than other areas of the stream. They make good midday resting spots for medium to large trout.

Brush piles offer good cover, break the current, and produce invertebrates for food. They usually hold small to medium trout.

Plunge pools are deep holes scoured out by falling water. They offer increased dissolved oxygen levels, and can be prime locations for good-sized trout.

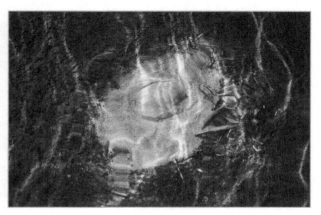

Upwelling springs appear as light spots of bubbling sand where the silt has been washed away. They draw trout in mid- to late summer.

Flats, slow-moving shallow areas, are morning and evening feeding areas. They normally lack the cover necessary to hold trout in midday.

Pocket water is shallow and has scattered boulders. It may appear too shallow, but the deep pockets below the boulders usually hold trout.

Typical Trout and Salmon Streams

Trout and salmon live in streams ranging in size from meadow brooks narrow enough to hop across, to major rivers large enough to carry oceangoing vessels. Described below are the most common types of trout and salmon streams, representing both the limestone and freestone categories:

FREESTONE STREAMS

Medium-gradient freestone streams, the most common trout stream type, have moderate current with numerous pools, riffles, and runs. The streambed is comprised mostly of large gravel, rubble, and boulders, and has some pocket water. Most medium-gradient freestone streams are fed by surface runoff and meltwater. Because the water carries few nutrients, these streams are relatively unproductive. However, many have large tributary systems that add enough nutrients to produce abundant food and large trout. The best of these streams have good spring flow, keeping water temperatures in the ideal range for trout feeding and growth.

High-gradient freestone streams, fed by snowmelt and surface runoff, are usually found in mountainous areas. The current is fast, with long stretches of pocket water but few pools. Because of the short food supply, trout usually run small but are willing biters.

Low-gradient freestone streams wind through bogs, meadows, or woodlands. They have sand or silt bottoms, and undercut banks or deadfalls for cover. Some, fed by springs or meltwater, have clear water; others, fed by swamp drainage, have tea-colored water.

LIMESTONE STREAMS

Low-gradient limestone streams have some spring flow, move slowly, and have a meandering streambed composed of silt, sand, or small gravel. The depth is fairly uniform, with few riffles. In meadow streams, a common variety, overhanging grass is the primary cover for trout.

Medium-gradient limestone streams normally have some spring flow, moderate to fast current, a pool-riffle-run configuration, and a streambed composed of gravel, rubble, or boulders. Many such streams flow over exposed limestone bedrock and have large numbers of crayfish.

OTHER COMMON STREAM TYPES

Tailwater streams, fed by cold water from the depths of a reservoir, produce trophy trout. The stream level may fluctuate greatly during the day as water is released to drive power turbines. This limits insect populations, but baitfish and crustaceans are plentiful.

Spring creeks, either limestone or freestone, arise from groundwater sources. They have slow to moderate current, very clear water, lush weed growth, and heavy insect populations. Some produce tremendous numbers of crustaceans and surprisingly large trout.

UNDERSTANDING MOVING WATER

Fast water in a riffle excavates a deeper channel, or run, immediately downstream. As current digs the run deeper, the velocity slows, forming a pool. Because of the slower current, sediment is deposited at the pool's downstream end, raising the streambed and channeling the water into a smaller area. Because the flow is more constricted, the current speeds up, forming another riffle. The sequence then repeats.

Why does a trout lie upstream of a boulder when there is a noticeable eddy on the downstream side? Why does it choose a feeding station on the bottom when most of its food is drifting on the surface? And why does a fly cast near the bank drift more slowly than a fly line in midstream?

Questions like these have a direct bearing on your ability to find and catch trout. Answering them correctly requires a basic understanding of stream hydraulics. The trout lies on the upstream side of the boulder because an eddy forms upstream of an object, as well as downstream.

The trout chooses a feeding station on the bottom because friction with bottom materials slows the current to as little as one-fourth the speed of the surface current. Similarly, the fly next to the bank drifts more slowly than the fly line in midstream because friction with the bank slows the current.

Understanding how moving water shapes the stream channel, and learning to recognize the resulting habitat types can also improve your chances of finding trout. In most good trout streams, the current creates a riffle-run-pool sequence that repeats itself along the stream course.

A deep pool may hold big brown trout, but rainbows and smaller browns are more likely to be found in runs. Riffles hold only small

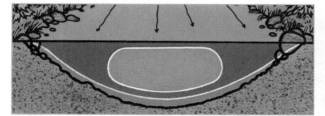

Current speed varies within the stream cross-section. The blue area has slow current; the purple, moderate current; the red, fast current. Water in the fast zone moves up to four times as fast as water in the slow zone.

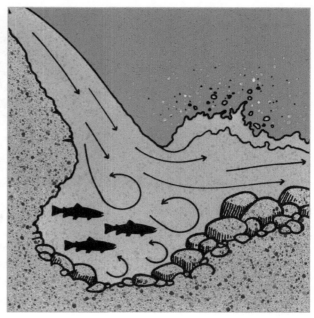

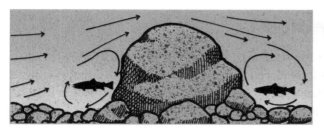

Eddies form both upstream and downstream of an obstacle such as a boulder. Many anglers do not realize that there is an eddy on the upstream side; they work only the downstream eddy, bypassing a lot of trout.

Plunge pools form at the base of a falls as a result of the cascading water. Plunge-pool depth usually exceeds the distance from the crest of the falls to the water level. A dugout often forms at the base of the falls.

trout during midday, but are important morning and evening feeding areas for most species. A normal stream tends to meander, or weave, as it flows downstream. Current flowing to the outside of a bend becomes swifter, eroding the streambed and sometimes carving an undercut bank. At the same time, current on the opposite side of the stream slackens, causing silt to settle out and fill in the streambed. In almost all cases, the outside bends hold the most trout.

Most stream fishermen know that water plunging over a falls digs out a pool at the base. But many do not realize that the turbulence caused by the plunging water undercuts the base of the falls, forming a cave that makes one of the best feeding and resting stations in the stream.

PARTS OF A STREAM

RIFFLE: Shallow water; fast current; turbulent surface; gravel, rubble, or boulder bottom. In big rivers, these areas are called rapids.

RUN: Deeper than a riffle, with moderate to fast current; surface not as turbulent; bottom materials range from small gravel to rubble.

POOL: Deep, slow-moving water with a flat surface; bottom of silt, sand, or small gravel. Similar but shallower areas are called flats.

Boils form when the current deflects upward off an underwater obstruction, usually a boulder. When you see a boil, there is a good chance that trout are holding in the eddy just downstream of the obstruction. But the boil forms farther downstream, so you must cast well upstream of the boil to catch the trout.

Reading Water

An experienced stream fisherman can learn a great deal about a stream simply by walking its banks and "reading" the water. He observes current patterns, surface disturbances, coloration differences, changes in bottom type, and other clues that reveal trout and salmon hiding spots.

Current patterns pinpoint the location of rocks, logs, or other underwater objects that shelter fish from the moving water. Current pushing against a bank may indicate an undercut that offers cover. The seam between fast and slow current makes a good feeding station; trout hold in the slower water waiting for food to drift by in the faster water.

Novice stream fishermen often pass up any water where the surface is broken and ripply, mistakenly assuming it is too fast and too shallow for trout. However, if you look carefully, you may see that this water has slack-water pockets. A small pocket behind a rock might be home to a good-sized trout, even though the water is less than a foot (30 cm) deep.

Bottom makeup also dictates where trout will be found. A section of stream with a sandy bottom generally supports fewer trout than a section with a rocky or gravelly bottom. Important trout foods, especially larval aquatic insects, thrive among rocks and gravel, but may be completely absent in sand.

If possible, examine the stream from a high angle to get an idea of streambed contour and location of boulders, submerged logs, weed patches, and other underwater objects. You can see best on a bright day when the sun is at its highest. Polarized sunglasses will remove the glare so you can see into the water.

Many trout streams have been damaged by erosion, beaver activity, channelization, or logging. Natural resources agencies and sportsmen's clubs sometimes reclaim these streams by installing devices to deepen the channel and provide good cover for trout.

Undercut banks can be found by watching the current. If it is angling toward a bank, rather than flowing parallel to it, the bank is undercut.

Deep holes appear as dark areas in the streambed. Trout move into holes to escape the current. The best holes have boulders or logs for cover.

Weed patches may be difficult to see, especially in low light. But the weeds usually slow the current, creating slack spots on the surface.

Current seams are easy to spot because debris and foam usually collect in the slack water, near the edge of the fast water.

Check your favorite stream at low-water stage to find deep holes and objects like submerged logs that could hold trout when the water is higher.

COMMON STREAM-IMPROVEMENT DEVICES

Crib shelters, man-made undercut banks supported by pilings, are built along outside bends. Water is deflected toward them by a rock or log structure on the opposite bank, scouring the bank under the crib. The left photo shows the shelter under construction, the right photo a year later.

Hewitt Ramps, used mainly on high-gradient streams, function much like small dams. A deeper pool forms above; a scour hole forms below.

WEATHER

Light rain or moderate wind disturbs the surface enough that trout cannot see you clearly. The fish feed heavily on terrestrial foods washed in by the rain or wind and are not nearly as spooky as they are when the surface is calm. But heavy rain pelting the surface or intense wind puts the trout down.

In stream fishing for trout and salmon, nothing is more important than weather. It affects the clarity, temperature, and water level of the stream, which largely determine where the fish will be found and how well they will bite.

The most important factor is rain. Trout often start to feed when the sky darkens before a storm. A light to moderate rain slightly clouds the water, washes terrestrial foods into the stream, increases the flow, and causes greater numbers of immature aquatic insects to drift downstream. These changes make ideal feeding conditions and good fishing. A heavy rain, on the other hand, seems to turn the fish off. If the downpour is prolonged, it muddies the water so much that the fish cannot see, and with the rising water, they abandon their normal locations.

Rain has even more effect on anadromous trout and salmon. Fish entering a stream to spawn tend to stage up at the stream mouth. A few will enter a stream at the normal flow, but the majority wait for the increased flow resulting from a heavy rain. Fishing is poor as long as the stream stays muddy, but improves rapidly when the water starts to clear.

Air temperature also has a dramatic effect on feeding activity. Most trout and salmon species feed heaviest at water temperatures from 55 to 60°F (12.8 to 15.6°C). On a typical stream, warm, sunny weather early or late in the season will drive the water temperature to that range by midafternoon, triggering an insect hatch and starting a feeding spree. But in summer the same type of weather warms the water too much by midafternoon, so fishing is poor. Then, trout bite better in the morning or evening, when the water is cooler.

Another important element is cloud cover. In sunny weather, trout are extra wary, seeking the cover of boulders, logs, or undercut banks. In cloudy weather, they are more aggressive and more willing to leave cover to find food. Anadromous fish tend to migrate more under cloudy skies.

Windy weather also makes trout more aggressive. The wind blows insects into the stream and the trout start feeding. However, trout have difficulty spotting small insects when the surface is choppy, so dry-fly fishing is not as effective as it would be if the water were calm.

GOOD CONDITIONS FOR TROUT FISHING

Overcast skies eliminate harsh shadows that can spook trout. The fish do not hesitate to leave cover to search for food, sometimes moving into riffles in midday.

Slightly murky water allows trout to see the lure, but makes it difficult for them to see you. The clarity is best when the stream is rising or after it starts to fall.

Chapter 2
EQUIPMENT

Whether you're fishing with fly or spinning gear, having the right equipment can make the difference between a successful fishing trip and a disappointing one. But choosing the right gear doesn't have to be difficult, and shouldn't keep you from pursuing trout and salmon.

In this section you'll learn how to choose the proper fly line, select the right fly rod and reel, and select the right leader. You'll also learn how to choose the right spinning or baitcasting rod, reel and line.

Next, we'll show you how to identify and select the appropriate accessories and tools to help you perform the little tasks such as adding tippet, weighting nymphs, keeping dry flies afloat, and checking water temperature.

Last, you'll learn how to choose waders and wading gear, including boots and wading accessories. We'll show you the various materials and styles of waders, and when and where to use each style.

Choosing the right fishing gear shouldn't be intimidating. In fact, it's the first step toward actually getting out on the water.

FLY RODS AND REELS

Rods

In spinning and baitcasting, it's important to select the right rod, but the selection is not as critical as in fly fishing. A fly rod propels the line, which in turn propels the fly; if the rod is not matched to the line, casting is next to impossible. When choosing a fly rod, consider the following:

MATERIAL. In the late 1940s, fiberglass rods revolutionized fly fishing. They were considerably less expensive than the old bamboo rods, yet lighter and stiffer, so they could handle a fly line more easily. With the introduction of graphite in 1972, rod-building technology took another quantum leap.

Today's graphite rods weigh 20 to 25 percent less than glass rods of the same stiffness, and 40 to 45 percent less than bamboo. Consequently, graphite rods can be longer and lighter, yet more powerful. And you can cast farther with less effort.

Because of the obvious advantages of graphite, fewer and fewer glass rods are produced these days. For those who enjoy the romance of fishing with a bamboo rod, there are many manufacturers and custom rod makers still building them. Some old bamboo rods have become collector items, commanding prices well into the thousands of dollars. Bamboo has enjoyed resurgence in popularity over the last decade or two, and it's doubtful bamboo rods ever will go out of style.

POWER. For peak casting performance, the power or stiffness of your fly rod should match the weight of your fly line. If the rod is too light, it will flex too much and lose its casting power. Too heavy, and it will not flex enough to propel the line.

Most fly rods have a line weight printed near the grip. As a rule, you can use line one size lighter or heavier than the recommended weight.

ROD ACTION. The word "action" may be the most misused term among fishermen. Some confuse action with power; others say "this rod has a nice action," meaning that it feels good in the hand.

In reality, two different characteristics determine "action." The first is where the rod bends under a load. The second is how quickly it recovers from a bend, or dampens. These characteristics are determined by the design of the taper of the rod, and the material with which the rod is made. Slow-action rods bend almost throughout their entire length, and recover slowly from a bend. Fast-action rods flex most near the tip, and recover quickly from a bend. In most cases, the fastest-action bamboo rod will feel considerably slower than even a slow-action graphite rod.

A faster rod forms a narrower loop, which travels more rapidly and has less air resistance, resulting in greater distance and accuracy. Faster rods also "dampen" more quickly after the cast, so the tip doesn't bounce and throw waves into the line. Waves in the line increase air resistance, reduce distance, and cause a sloppy delivery.

A slower rod absorbs more shock, a big advantage when fishing dry flies with light tippets. A slower rod makes it easier to control casting distance. Because the loop is not as narrow, the line speed is slower, so you can easily stop the line when the fly is over the target. Nonetheless, the wide loop reduces casting distance considerably.

Unfortunately, there are no industry standards to designate action, and some rod makers don't even try. One manufacturer's "slow" rod may have the same action as another's "medium" rod. An experienced tackle-shop employee can help you make your decision.

LENGTH. A 7½- to 9-foot (2.3 to 2.7 m) fly rod suits most trout fishing situations, but longer and shorter rods also have their uses.

In the past, fishermen shied away from longer rods because they were too heavy. Today's graphite rods are so light that greater lengths are becoming popular. Long rods give you more casting power, make it easier to mend the line, and help you keep your back cast high enough to avoid streamside brush. Also, with the rod tip high it's easier to control your line and fly on the drift. Salmon anglers often use two-handed rods called Spey rods, named for Scotland's legendary Spey River, up to 15 feet (4.6 m) in length, for making long casts, controlling the line on the water, and handling these powerful fish.

Short rods are easier to handle on narrow, brushy streams. They also make it easier to place a fly beneath an overhang, and to land trout in tight spots. Anglers on brush-lined creeks sometimes use fly rods as short as 6 feet (1.8 m).

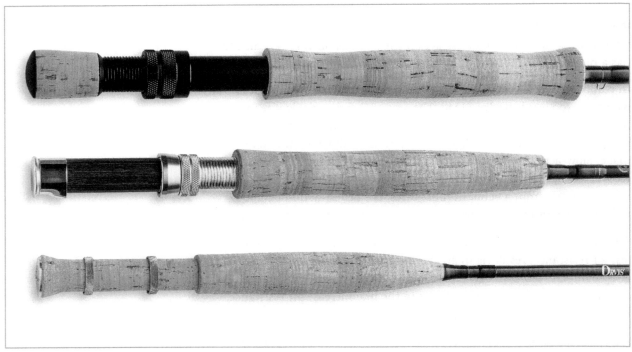

Reel seats include (top) down-locking, used on light rods; (middle) up-locking, used on heavier rods to prevent unscrewing, and for more length behind the reel so the spool won't rub clothing; (bottom) sliding-band, to reduce weight on bamboo rods and light graphite rods.

Grips include (top) cigar, for short- to medium-range casting with light rods; (middle) half Wells, with a thicker front for more casting leverage and a raised middle for a better grip; (bottom) full Wells, with a raised front for even more casting leverage, and a raised middle.

Reels

Choosing a fly reel is not nearly as complicated as choosing the right fly rod or line. The reel serves primarily to store the line, and to provide drag tension when a fish makes a long run. When selecting a fly reel, consider the following:

REEL ACTION. The action of a reel is the way it retrieves line. With a single-action reel, the spool turns once for each turn of the handle; with a multiplying reel, it turns more than once.

Single-action reels are adequate for most trout fishing. Multiplying reels, though heavier, are better for powerful fish like steelhead. They allow you to take up slack in a hurry should a fish run toward you. Both actions are highly reliable.

Both types of reels are also available in direct-drive and anti-reverse models. Direct drives are more common; the handle turns when the spool does, so if a big fish takes line, the handle turns backward. Should you accidentally touch the whirling handle, your tippet would snap. On anti-reverse models, the handle does not turn backward with the spool.

DRAG. When a big trout grabs your fly and rockets away, you'll need a good drag to prevent spool overrun, and to tire the fish. The simplest type of drag is the ratchet-and-pawl. An adjustable spring keeps the pawl pressed against the ratchet and makes an audible click. Disc-style drags perform like the brakes on a car, using smooth friction of one large surface against another. Both are adjusted with a knob on the side of the reel. Many reels have an exposed spool rim, which allows you to apply additional drag tension by pressing your palm against the rim, called palming.

CAPACITY AND WEIGHT. The reel you choose should be designed to hold the size fly line you've selected with ample capacity for backing material. The larger the fish you're after, the greater the capacity you'll need. Check the capacity information listed in the literature that comes with the reel to be sure it can hold the required line and backing.

ARBOR. The arbor is the center axis of the reel spool, to which you tie the backing. Once the backing has filled the reel to the proper capacity, the fly line is tied to the backing, and the balance of the reel is filled. Fly reels traditionally have had a narrow center axis, or arbor. Reel designers discovered that by increasing the diameter and width of the reel's arbor, the reel takes up line more quickly. These reels, called "large-arbor," are popular with anglers pursuing large trout and salmon. Mid-arbor reels combine the added backing capacity of traditional narrow-arbor reels with the faster take-up of large arbor reels, and are most common on big-game reels.

Most fly reels will accommodate a range of line weights.

FLY LINE

The fly line distinguishes fly fishing from all other forms of fishing, and makes it possible to cast an essentially weightless fly. The weight of the line bends, or loads, the rod, propelling the line, leader, and fly.

A well-stocked tackle shop offers a wide assortment of fly lines. They come in different weights, different tapers, and a selection of colors. Some float, some sink, and some do a little of each. Choosing the right lines for various situations need not be difficult. Your decision depends mainly on the weight designation of your fly rod, and the size of your fly. It also depends on how far you want to cast, and how deep you want to fish. Other factors that may influence your selection include the trout's wariness, the water's surface (smooth or broken), and the amount of wind.

Most fly lines are 80 to 100 feet (24.4 to 30.5 m) long, consisting of a core of braided nylon or Dacron with a plastic coating. The plastic may be impregnated with tiny air bubbles or metal powder to make it float or sink, and it may vary in thickness so that the line tapers. When selecting and using fly lines, consider the following:

LINE WEIGHT. Every fly line is designed to conform to precise weight standards set by the tackle industry. This means that every 5-weight line—whether it sinks or floats—weighs exactly the same over the first 30 feet (9.1 m) of the line. This precise weight designation assures rod manufacturers that each of their rods can be designed to cast a specific weight line. Line weight is measured in grains, an ancient British measurement based on the weight of a grain of barley.

Practically all trout and salmon fishing is done with line weights 2 to 12.

Light-weight lines (2 to 4) give you the most delicate presentation. With line this light you can cast small, unweighted flies, but you cannot cast as far, and casting in a strong wind may be difficult.

Medium-weight lines (5 to 7) are the most versatile. They can handle flies of almost any size, and perform well in most fishing situations.

Heavy-weight lines (8 and 9) can deliver large flies and punch through the wind. Shooting-head lines are most often used in weights of 8 or heavier.

Extra-heavy lines (10 to 15) are used mainly for steelhead and salmon. Most lead-core shooting heads do not carry standard weight designations, but usually are cast with 10-weight rods. In Europe, anglers use 11- and 12-weight lines with two-handed salmon rods, but these are less popular in North America.

LINE TAPER. A fly line that tapers, or varies in diameter along its length, casts more efficiently than a level line. The forward section, or front taper, is thin at the tip but expands to a thicker section called the belly. The length and position of the belly determine how far and how delicately a given line will cast.

FLY LINE NUMBER DESIGNATION AND WEIGHT IN GRAINS		
Number Designation	**Standard Weight in grains** (grams)	
1-Weight	60	(3.89 g)
2-Weight	80	(5.18 g)
3-Weight	100	(6.48 g)
4-Weight	120	(7.78 g)
5-Weight	140	(9.07 g)
6-Weight	160	(10.36 g)
7-Weight	185	(11.98 g)
8-Weight	210	(13.61 g)
9-Weight	240	(15.55 g)
10-Weight	280	(18.14 g)
11-Weight	330	(21.38 g)
12-Weight	380	(24.62 g)
13-Weight	450	(29.16 g)
14-Weight	500	(32.40 g)
15-Weight	550	(35.64 g)

With weight-forward (WF) line, the belly is short and near the forward end, so it shoots out easily, pulling the thinner running line with it. Weight-forward lines are the best choice for beginners. They are good for distance casting, but do not roll cast well.

On double-taper (DT) line, the belly is long and in the middle of the line; both ends taper equally. A double-taper line does not cast as far as a weight-forward, but is easier to mend and more economical; you can reverse it when one end wears out.

The shooting head or shooting taper (ST) is a special-purpose line that consists of about 30 feet (9.1 m) of level or tapered fly line, loop-spliced to 100 feet (30.5 m) of 15- to 30-pound (6.8 to 13.6 kg) mono running line. The mono is usually flattened or oval-shaped to minimize coiling. The heavy head easily pulls the mono, so you can cast extreme distances. They lack delicacy, and the long running line tangles easily. To minimize tangling, use a shooting basket or substitute a special thin fly line for the mono. Using the thin fly line reduces casting distance.

BUOYANCY. Floating lines (designated by the letter F) are the obvious choice for fishing dry flies. Because the line floats high on the surface film, little effort is required to pick it up for another cast, or to mend it. Floating lines can also be used with sinking flies, with or without added weight such as split shot or lead leader-wrap. With a floating line and a long leader, you can fish a sinking fly several feet (m) down.

Sinking lines (S) come in different densities, ranging from slow sinking to extremely fast sinking, for different depths, current speeds, and retrieve speeds. Because they sink over their entire length, they are difficult to control in current, and you must retrieve most of the line in order to make another cast. As a rule, use a sinking line whenever you are fishing deeper than 10 feet (3 m).

Sink tip lines, also called floating/sinking lines (F/S), have 5 to 20 feet (1.5 to 6.1 m) of sinking line attached to a floating line. Generally, the sinking portion is a different color. The sink rate of the tip ranges from

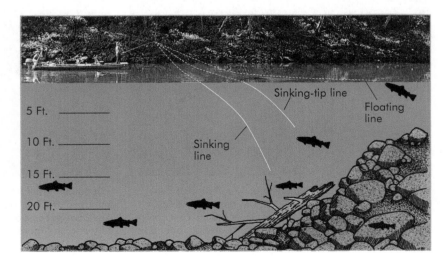

intermediate to extremely fast. Because only the tip sinks, these lines are easier than sinking lines to pick up from the water. They work well at depths of 2 to 10 feet (0.61 to 3 m).

LINE DESIGNATIONS. When you purchase a fly line, look for a three-part code on the label that designates the taper, weight, and flotation of the line. The code WF-06-F, for instance, designates a weight-forward, 6-weight, floating fly line.

MATCHING ROD TO LINE. The weight of your line determines the power of the rod needed to handle it. If you try to cast a light line with a heavy rod, the rod will not flex enough to load. If you try to cast a heavy line with a light rod, the rod will flex too much to propel it. Most rods, however, will handle a line one weight either side of the recommended weight.

Backing helps prevent a fish from running out all your fly line.

Unfortunately, there is no standard way to measure rod power, so considerable variation exists among manufacturers. A 7-weight rod from one manufacturer may have the same power as a 5-weight rod from another. A good fly-fishing shop can help you sort out these differences.

Another complication is that line weight is measured by the weight of only the front 30 feet (9.1 m); no consideration is given to the rest of the line. The middle portion of a double-taper line, for instance, is thicker and heavier than the same portion of a weight-forward line. So you should select a double-taper line one size lighter than a weight-forward line for the same rod.

LINE COLOR. The color of a fly line is a matter of personal preference. Some fly casters prefer floating lines in bright colors because they are easiest to see, while others choose lines in subtle grays and greens to avoid spooking trout in clear spring creeks. Sinking lines, however, usually come in various shades of brown, green, or gray. In most types of fly fishing, the leader is long enough that the fish do not notice the color of the line.

BACKING. To keep a big fish from running out all your line, always use backing under your fly line. Backing also keeps your spool full so you can reel up line more quickly, and it minimizes coiling. Most trout fishermen use 20-pound (9 kg) braided Dacron.

Most reel manufacturers print the recommended amount of backing for each line weight right on the box, to take the guesswork out of spooling on the backing.

LINE CARE. If your line gets dirty or oily, simply wash it with mild soap. Floating lines need more care; use a commercial line cleaner to condition them. The line will stay pliable, float better, and shoot through the guides easier. Store your line where it will not be exposed to sunlight. Practice casting on grass or water; pavement will scuff your line. Gasoline and insect repellent can also damage the line's surface.

FLY LEADERS

The leader creates a nearly invisible connection between the heavy fly line and the fly. It also transfers the energy of the cast smoothly and efficiently, and helps give the fly a lifelike action on or in the water. The following components are important in leader selection.

MATERIAL. Until the 1950s, fly leaders were made from silkworm gut, which was strong and had low visibility, but became stiff and brittle when dry. Gut leaders required overnight soaking to make them supple enough for fishing.

Modern leaders come in a variety of man-made materials, which require far less care.

Nylon monofilament, the most popular leader material, is inexpensive, durable, and nearly invisible, with excellent knot strength. However, monofilament breaks down quickly in sunlight, and absorbs water, causing it to weaken.

Polyvinylidene fluoride (PVDF) material, commonly called "fluorocarbon," is even less visible in water than nylon, because its refractive properties, or the way light rays bend as they pass through it, more closely match the refractive properties of water. It has greater abrasion resistance but less stretch, requiring a more gentle hookset to prevent break offs with light tippets. Fluorocarbon is not affected by sunlight, and it will not absorb water. However, it costs more and has poorer knot strength than mono.

TAPER. Most leaders taper from a relatively thick butt section to a fine tippet. This taper ensures that the leader turns over easily and presents only the narrow-diameter tippet to the fish.

Fly leaders consist of a gradually tapering butt (about 60 percent of leader length), a rapidly tapering transition section (about 20 percent of length), and a level tip section or tippet (about 20 percent of length).

Modern tapered leaders come in two styles: knotted and knotless. A knotted leader normally has three to eight sections of monofilament of different diameters, tied together with blood knots. To ensure that the energy of the cast is transferred smoothly from line to leader, the thickest part of the leader butt should measure 0.017 inch (0.04 cm) for 2- to 4-weight fly line, 0.019 inch (0.048 cm) for 5- to 7-weight line, and 0.021 inch (0.053 cm) for line weights of 8 or over. For good knot strength, adjacent sections should differ in diameter by no more than 0.002 inch (0.0051 cm).

A knotted leader can be modified to suit your needs, and worn sections can be cut out and new ones tied in. However, the knots will weaken the leader and may pick up bits of weeds or debris.

Knotless leaders, by far the most popular, are stronger and do not catch debris. But if they do not have the right taper to turn over smoothly, there is little you can do but tie on a different leader.

With any leader, the tippet becomes shorter as new flies are tied on and worn sections are cut off. Rather than replacing the whole leader when the tippet becomes too short, simply replace the tippet. You can buy tippet material in 25-yard (22.9 m) spools.

HOW TO MAKE A KNOTTED LEADER

Taper Butt
(60 percent of
leader length)

Transition Section
(20 percent of
leader length)

Tippet
(20 percent of
leader length)

Fly

LENGTH. The length of your leader depends on the type of fly you plan to use. A sinking fly, when fished with a sinking or sink tip line, requires a short leader, from 3 to 4 feet (0.9 to 1.2 m). Strikes on sinking flies may be difficult to detect, and a short leader gives you a more direct connection. A short leader also pulls the fly deeper. A dry or sinking fly fished with a floating line requires a long leader, from 7½ to 12 feet (2.3 to 3.7 m).

With dry flies, the long leader can be manipulated to alight in a series of S-curves. This way, the fly floats freely for a longer time before drag sets in. A long tippet is especially important to ensure a drag-free drift.

TIPPET DIAMETER. A tippet's diameter is measured using a system developed in the days of silkworm gut leaders. The gut was drawn through a series of decreasing-size holes in metal plates, reducing its diameter. Each draw earned it another X (or mathematical times symbol; in other words, "4X" meant "drawn four times"). Even today, a tippet's X rating indicates diameter, not its breaking strength; the same X-rating may have different strengths depending on the manufacturer and material. The higher the X-rating number, the smaller the diameter.

The proper tippet diameter depends on the size of your fly. Always use the lightest tippet that will cast the fly efficiently.

Leader length and tippet diameter also depend on the size of the stream, the clarity of the water, and the wind conditions, as well as the size and wariness of the fish. On a very small stream or in windy weather, you may need a shorter-than-normal leader. On a very clear stream, or when trout are extra wary, your leader should be longer than normal. A heavy tippet improves your chances of landing a big trout, but reduces your odds of getting the fish to strike in the first place.

LEADER CARE. Mono leaders require little care, but you should store them in a lightproof package and check their strength and pliability before using. Heat, sunlight, or fluorescent light can weaken the leader and make it brittle. Check your leader often for nicks and abrasion. Replace your leader or tippet section if it develops a wind knot or abrasion. A small knot can reduce line strength by as much as 50 percent.

TIPPET SIZE CHART			
Tippet Size	**Diameter in Inches**	**Fly Size**	**Pound Test**
0X	0.011 (0.0279 cm)	2-1/0	6.5–15.5 (2.95–7.05 kg)
1X	0.010 (0.0254 cm)	2-6	5.5–13.5 (2.5–6.14 kg)
2X	0.009 (0.0229 cm)	4-8	4.5–11.5 (2.05–5.23 kg)
3X	0.008 (0.0203 cm)	8-12	3.8–8.5 (1.73–3.86 kg)
4X	0.007 (0.0178 cm)	10-14	3.1–5.5 (1.41–2.5 kg)
5X	0.006 (0.0152 cm)	12-16	2.4–4.5 (1.09–2.05 kg)
6X	0.005 (0.0127 cm)	16-20	1.4–3.5 (0.5–1.59 kg)
7X	0.004 (0.0102 cm)	20-24	1.1–2.5 (0.5–1.14 kg)
8X	0.003 (0.0076 cm)	24-28	0.75–1.75 (0.75–1.75 kg)

Tippets of the same diameter vary in strength depending on the brand of monofilament.

SPINNING AND BAITCASTING TACKLE

Stream trout anglers use a variety of spinning and baitcasting tackle for fishing hardware and natural-bait rigs. Here are some guidelines for selecting rods, reels, and line:

Rods

All graphite rods are not the same. Some have considerably higher graphite content, and there are different types of graphite materials. You will get noticeably better performance from rods made of extra stiff, or high modulus, graphite. The rods most commonly used in stream trout fishing include:

LIGHT SPINNING. In small streams, fishermen commonly use light to ultralight spinning rods with 2- to 6-pound (0.9 to 2.7 kg) mono. Most rods for this type of fishing measure 4½ to 5½ feet (1.37 to 1.67 m) in length, have a medium action, and are designed for lures from ⅟32 to ⅜ ounce (0.89 g to 10.6 g). A medium-action rod flexes enough to cast most light lures and baits, yet has enough backbone for a good hookset. To cast extremely light lures, you need a slow-action rod.

MEDIUM SPINNING. These work best in medium to large streams with good-sized trout. They will easily handle ¼- to ⅝-ounce (7.1 to 17.7 g) lures, which are needed for adequate casting distance and getting to the bottom. A typical outfit for this situation includes a 6- to 7-foot (1.8 to 2.1 m) medium-action rod and 6- to 8-pound (2.7 to 3.6 kg) mono.

Light spinning gear works well on small streams where brush or trees restrict your casting motion. A sidearm or backhand casting stroke places your lure beneath the branches.

Medium spinning gear is the best choice for wider, deeper, or faster-moving streams. Here, heavier lures are often necessary to make long casts and to reach bottom in the swift current.

Salmon and steelhead gear is needed to handle large salmonids in big rivers. The long, stiff rod gives you extra casting distance and more leverage for turning a powerful fish.

STEELHEAD AND SALMON. A long, stiff rod, combined with a high-capacity reel, is ideal for casting long distances. This type of rod also gives you more control of the line, better sensitivity, and more power for tiring the fish.

Some rod manufacturers now produce a line of steelhead and salmon rods that includes both spinning and baitcasting models. Most of these rods measure 8 to 10 feet (2.44 to 3.05 m) in length. They will handle lures from ½ to 2 ounces (14.2 to 56.7 g) and mono from 10- to 20-pound (4.5 to 9.1 kg) test. For drift fishing, steelhead and salmon fishermen often match an 8- to 9-foot (2.4 to 2.7 m) fly rod with a spinning reel.

Reels

Make sure your spinning reel has a large-diameter spool and a smooth drag. On many spinning reels, the spool is so small that even limp mono tends to coil. For a light or ultralight rod, spool diameter should be at least 1½ inches (3.8 cm); for a medium-power rod, 1¾ inches (4.5 cm); for a steelhead rod, 2 inches (5.1 cm).

A smooth drag is important in any stream fishing; if your drag sticks, even a small trout can snap your line in fast current. As a rule, front drags are smoother than rear drags. If possible, test the drag by attaching a 6- to 8-ounce (170 to 227 g) weight to the line, lifting the weight off the ground, then gradually loosening the drag. The weight should drop slowly and evenly; if it drops in jerks, look for another reel.

The drag is equally important on a baitcasting reel. Cheap reels often have "all-or-nothing" drags. When set light, the drag slips so much you can't set the hook. If you tighten it, it grabs too much and a big fish will break your line.

LINE. Trout are extremely line-shy, so most anglers use clear mono, or mono shaded to match the color of the water. Fluorescent line or other high-visibility line is not recommended. Hard-finish lines are popular for drift fishing because they can take more abrasion, but they're too stiff for most trout fishing. Limp mono works better for casting light lures and baits; it has less memory, meaning it is not as likely to form coils that reduce casting distance. But limp mono nicks easier, so you must retie hooks and lures more often.

TROUT FISHING ACCESSORIES

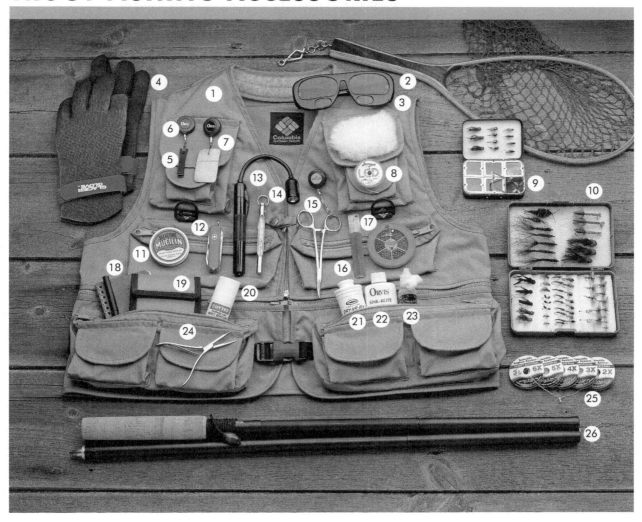

When you're wading a trout stream, you may walk a mile (1.6 km) or more from your starting point. Should you forget something, it's a long walk back to your car. To avoid such problems, wear a fishing vest with lots of pockets and carry your accessories with you. You probably won't need all the accessories described below, but this list may give you some ideas.

CLIPPERS. Ordinary fingernail clippers will work for cutting line, but specially designed clippers are much better. They stay sharper longer, and have a small pin for cleaning head cement out of the eyes of fly hooks.

CREEL. Canvas or wicker creels are best; when you wet them, evaporation keeps the fish cool.

Trout fishing accessories include: (1) fishing vest, (2) landing net with French snap, (3) polarized sunglasses, (4) neoprene gloves, (5) line clipper on (6) retractor reel, (7) leader straightener on retractor, (8) leader wrap, (9) fly box with spring-loaded lids, (10) large, foam-lined fly box, (11) floatant, (12) Swiss Army knife, (13) gooseneck light, (14) water thermometer, (15) forceps on retractor, (16) hook file, (17) split shot assortment, (18) notebook and pen, (19) leader wallet, (20) insect repellent, (21) silicone fly desiccant, (22) leader sink, (23) fly line cleaner, (24) needle-nose pliers, (25) tippet material, (26) wading staff.

FINGERLESS GLOVES. These gloves keep your hands warm and dry, yet allow you to tie knots. The warmest ones are made of neoprene.

FLY BOX. Fly fishermen often carry several fly boxes. Dry flies should be stored in a box with large compartments to avoid crushing the delicate hackle. A simple plastic box with a tight-fitting lid and good-sized compartments will do, but a box that has compartments with individual spring-loaded lids protects your flies better from wind and rain.

With other flies, the type of box is less critical. Some boxes have metal clips to hold the flies, but the clips are usually too large to hold flies smaller than size 14. Some boxes are magnetic, and in others the flies are embedded in foam; the foam boxes are best for tiny flies.

Traditional fleece-lined fly books are still used, but if a fly is stored wet, the fleece absorbs moisture, and the hook rusts.

FLOATANT. Silicone floatants in paste, liquid, or spray form will keep a dry fly floating longer.

FORCEPS. This tool is best for removing hooks from smaller trout.

HOOK HONE. Fly hooks are easily damaged by bumping rocks. The point can be resharpened with a small jewelry file or stone.

INSECT NET. A net is used to scoop insects from the water for identification. A small aquarium net will do. Some anglers carry small bottles so they can take the insects home for study.

INSECT REPELLENT. Stick repellent is best. Avoid lotion types that adhere to your hands; they could damage your fly line.

LANDING NET. Choose a net with a short handle and cotton mesh. Cotton is softer and less abrasive than synthetic material, so it's the best choice for catch-and-release fishing. Attach the net to your vest with a French clip, so you can detach it quickly.

LEADER SINK. Apply this to a leader so it sinks quickly when using wet flies or nymphs.

LEADER STRAIGHTENER. The most popular type of straightener is a piece of leather, lined with silicone-treated rubber. Squeeze your tippet in the rubber and pull it through to remove any kinks or curls.

LEADER WALLET. Use wallets for storing extra leaders. Choose a wallet with zip-lock plastic holders.

LEADER WRAP. The flat lead wire can be wrapped on your leader as a substitute for split shot.

LINE CLEANER. Remove dirt and oil from your fly line.

NEEDLE-NOSE PLIERS. Use this tool for removing hooks from large trout and for flattening barbs in catch-and-release fishing. Select a small, lightweight model, preferably made of stainless steel.

NOTEBOOK. Use a notebook to record information on insect hatches and other streamside observations that could be useful in future years.

POLARIZED GLASSES. Polarized glasses reduce glare so you can see both bottom features and fish. Glass lenses resist scratching better than plastic. Prescription polarized lenses are available at most eyewear stores. You can also get glasses with small magnifying lenses for examining small objects.

PRIEST. This small club is used for quickly killing trout you wish to keep.

RAIN JACKET. Keep a light rain parka in the large pocket on the back of your vest.

RETRACTOR REEL. This small reel has a retractable cord for attaching clippers, forceps, or other commonly used accessories. The reel pins to your vest.

SILICONE POWDER. This drying agent quickly removes water or fish slime from a dry fly and reshapes the hackle. Place your fly in the container and shake; the powder will absorb the water.

SPLIT SHOT. An assortment of split shot in small sizes is needed to take sinking flies deep. A fly with split shot 6 to 12 inches (15.2 to 30.5 cm) ahead of it swims more naturally than one with lead wire on the hook shank. Split shot are also used for drifting live bait.

STOMACH PUMP. A pump is used for extracting stomach contents from trout you wish to release. The pump is simply a plastic tube with a rubber squeeze-bulb at one end.

SWISS ARMY KNIFE. The knife blade can be used for gutting trout, the scissors for trimming hackle, the screwdriver for fixing a reel, the tweezers for examining insects, the toothpick for tying a nail knot.

TAPE MEASURE. For their personal records, many fishermen like to measure their trout before releasing them. Where length regulations apply, you may need to measure a trout to determine if it is legal size. A small tape measure will do, but you can also buy adhesive-backed tapes that stick to the butt section of your fly rod.

TIPPET MATERIAL. Carry tippet spools in all the diameters you normally use to rebuild leaders.

VEST. Your vest should have enough pockets to carry the gear you normally need for a day's fishing, including raingear. Look for a vest with zippers on the large pockets, Velcro fasteners on the small ones, and a ring or loop at the rear of the collar for attaching a landing net. Make sure the vest is large enough that you can wear a heavy sweater underneath. Short vests are available for wading in deep water, and vests with mesh backs and shoulders are available for hot weather.

VEST LIGHT. A light helps when changing flies, unhooking fish, and finding your way in the dark. Select one with a clip that attaches to your vest, and with a gooseneck for directing the light.

WADING STAFF. A staff helps keep your balance in fast current. Collapsible staffs made of aluminum tubing are easy to carry in your vest, but wooden staffs are also popular.

WATER THERMOMETER. Select a fast-registering thermometer, preferably one with a metal tube. Tie the tube to a cord long enough to reach the bottom.

Waders and Hip Boots

Modern materials have made waders lighter, tougher, safer, and more comfortable. The biggest improvement is the development of breathable waders. Made from a permeable membrane sandwiched between layers of durable yet lightweight nylon, breathable waders allow moisture such as perspiration or water to pass through the wader material into the river, keeping you cool and dry on warm days. Breathable waders are more expensive than waders made of neoprene or rubber, but are substantially lighter and more comfortable. And since most of the research and development in waders is focused on breathable technology, they are becoming more durable and less expensive.

In cold water fishing, neoprene waders still hold the edge. Neoprene is warm, remarkably durable, and flexible enough to mold to your body. If you fall into the water, your waders won't fill, and the closed-cell foam may help keep you afloat. Neoprene waders can be easily repaired with a special adhesive should they develop a leak. They do have a drawback: They're simply too warm for hot weather.

Nylon waders are better for warm-weather fishing. They come in stocking-foot or boot-foot models and are relatively inexpensive.

Hip boots are ideal for shallow streams. Most are made of rubber or rubber-impregnated canvas with a boot foot, although nylon models are available in stocking foot. Hip boots with a rubber-impregnated canvas or Cordura upper will wear better than all-rubber boots, and are more puncture-resistant.

Boot-foot waders come with the boots attached. They are convenient to put on, but the ankles fit loosely and offer little support. Some come with felt soles.

Stocking-foot waders fit more snugly, so they have less current resistance. Separate wading shoes provide ankle support; the felt soles improve traction on slippery rocks.

The growing popularity of fly fishing among women has led some manufacturers, such as Wright & McGill with their "Fly Girl" brand, to produce comfortable breathable waders designed specifically for female anglers.

Hip boots should fit snugly around the ankle and lower calf (left). If the ankle portion is too large (right), the boot will pull loose from your foot when you walk in the mud.

Stream cleats fit over your wading shoes and boot-foots. They give you more traction than felt soles on mossy rocks in fast current.

Gravel guards keep sand and rocks out of boots used with stocking-foot waders. Some waders have gravel guards built in.

Wading belts help keep water out of your waders should you fall.

Chapter 3
STREAM FISHING BASICS

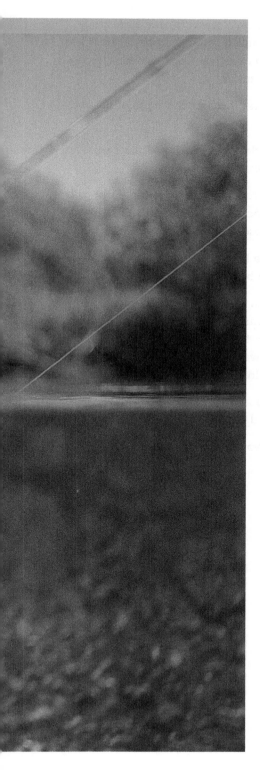

Trout are among the wariest of gamefish. Any quick movement or unusual sound, like the crunching of gravel or clattering of loose rocks when you wade, will send them darting for cover.

You can minimize spooking by following these guidelines:

- Keep a low profile; the lower you are, the less likely you will appear in the trout's window of vision. To fish a narrow stream, you may have to crawl to the bank and cast from a kneeling position.

- Wear drab clothing that blends in with the surroundings. A bright-colored shirt or cap can put the trout down in a hurry.

- In turbulent water, you can approach a trout more closely than in slow or slack water.

- Use objects such as boulders and trees to conceal your approach. If there is no place to hide, try to stay in the shadows.

- When you reach a likely spot, stand still for a few minutes before making a cast. When you first arrive, trout detect your presence and stop feeding. After a few minutes, they may get used to you and start to feed again, even if you are plainly visible.

- Try to avoid casting over the trout's window of vision, especially with bright-colored fly line.

WADING

In small, narrow streams, you will probably want to fish from the bank to conceal yourself, but you can fish most other streams more easily by wading. When you wade, your profile is lower, your back cast is less obstructed, and you can get closer to midstream lies. To wade effectively and safely, keep these suggestions in mind:

- Don't step off the bank without first checking the depth; if possible, cross at a riffle.

- Wear felt-soled waders or stream cleats for traction. Rubber soles are far too slippery for wading over wet, algae-covered rocks.

- Step softly to avoid banging rocks together. Before putting your full weight on a rock, make sure the rock is stable so it doesn't clink against other rocks or make you lose your balance.

- Walk with short, shuffling steps to keep ripples to a minimum on quiet pools, and to feel an uneven bottom better.

- In most situations, wade upstream. Trout face into the current, so you will be approaching them from behind and not stirring up silt that will drift over them. Also, it's safer to wade upstream; if you trip, the current helps hold you up. If you wade downstream, the current may push you too fast, causing you to lose your balance.

- To move from one spot to another along a stream, walk on the bank instead of wading in the streambed and disturbing the fish.

- Wear polarized glasses; they help you to spot fish and to avoid obstructions that could trip you.

TIPS FOR SAFE WADING

Carry a wading staff to help keep your balance in fast water or on a boulder-strewn bottom. A collapsible staff can be carried in your vest.

Turn sideways when wading in fast current. This minimizes the force of the current, so your feet are not swept out from under you.

Pivot upstream to turn around in fast current. If you pivot downstream, the current pushes you too fast, tending to wash you off your feet.

HOOKING, PLAYING AND LANDING TROUT

The light lines and leaders used by most trout fishermen can easily result in a break-off, unless you know how to hook, play, and land the fish properly.

Trout have comparatively soft mouths, so you do not have to set the hook hard. The fine-wire hooks on most flies and trout lures penetrate easily, assuming they're well-sharpened. Fly fishermen often make the mistake of jerking the rod too hard when a trout takes the fly, snapping the light tippet.

When you hook a trout, it usually makes a powerful initial run. Unless the fish heads for snaggy cover, don't try to stop it. With spinning tackle, make sure your drag is set on the light side. With a fly rod, let the reel handle spin freely; the clicker will prevent the line from overrunning. When you hook a large trout or salmon, it's a good idea to slow the run as soon as possible so the fish can't reach the rapids and swim into the next pool.

You may have to follow the fish if it takes too much line. After the initial run, start applying some pressure. Keep your rod tip high enough for the rod to absorb the force of a sudden run. If the fish jumps, quickly lower your rod tip to reduce the tension. Otherwise, a head shake could break your line. Don't let the fish rest; it will soon tire if you maintain steady pressure.

Small trout hooked on a fly rod can be landed by simply stripping in line, but with bigger trout it pays to use your reel so you have the advantage of a mechanical drag.

If possible, fly fishermen should keep their entire leader outside the tip-top during the fight. The line-to-leader connection could hang up in the guides should a trout make a last-minute run, and the tippet could snap. Using a needle knot rather than a nail knot will minimize the problem.

When you plan to release the fish, play it as quickly as possible. If the fight drags on, the fish may become too stressed to survive. A light tippet, while considered very sporting, results in a longer fight that may kill the trout. Even if it swims away, it may die later.

Net the fish, or beach it if you're near a gradually sloping bank. When you lead a trout into the shallows and it feels bottom, it often panics and beaches itself.

TIPS FOR HOOKING, PLAYING, AND LANDING TROUT ON FLIES

Wait until the trout sucks in a dry fly and closes its mouth before setting the hook. If you try to set too soon, you'll pull the fly out of its mouth.

Palm the spool of an exposed-rim fly reel for extra drag. This keeps a big steelhead or salmon from getting into a rapids and running too far downstream.

Set the hook by lifting the rod with a stiff wrist while stripping in line with your other hand. Lift the rod tip straight up rather than pulling back.

Keep your net out of the water while the trout is still "green." Putting the net into the water before the fish tires may cause it to dart away.

Net the trout headfirst when it tires, plunging the net under it quickly. To keep the fish from breaking off in the net, slacken the line as you lift.

Avoid chasing the trout with your net. If you attempt to net the trout tail-first, it may feel the net and surge forward, breaking your line.

CATCH-AND-RELEASE

Production of trout can be measured like production of crops. Just as farmers record crop yields in bushels per acre (0.4 ha), fisheries managers record trout yields in pounds (kg) per acre (0.4 ha).

Hat Creek, a heavily fished California stream, produces about 60 pounds (27.3 kg) of trout per acre (0.4 ha) per year. In 1983, a creel census was conducted on a 3½-mile (5.6 km) stretch of the stream, which had a total annual production estimated at 2800 pounds (1272.7 kg) of trout. In that year, fishermen caught over 20,000 pounds (9,090.9 kg) of trout, over seven times the productive capacity of the stream. Fortunately, most of these fish were released. It's obvious that this stream could not continue to provide good fishing for the entire season unless fishermen returned a good share of their trout to the water.

Heavy fishing pressure on some popular streams has prompted conservation agencies to install catch-and-release regulations. And even where such regulations are not in effect, more and more fishermen are voluntarily returning most of their trout.

There's no disputing the concept of catch-and-release fishing, but unless fishermen know exactly how to release their fish, many will die from mishandling. If you follow the procedure shown on the next page, the trout and salmon you release will have an excellent chance of survival.

Flatten your barbs so you can remove hooks without injuring the fish. By keeping a tight line during the fight, you will seldom lose a fish.

Move to a location out of the current to play the fish. This way, it cannot use the current to its advantage, so it tires more quickly.

Leave the fish in the water, grasp the hook with a pliers or hemostat, then gently shake the hook to release the fish. This way, you won't remove the protective slime.

Cut the leader if a fish is deeply hooked. In a Wisconsin study, 56 percent of deep-hooked trout survived when the leader was cut; 11 percent when the hook was removed.

Hold the fish in an upright position facing into the current. Give it time to recover so it can swim away on its own. If it starts to sink, hold it upright a while longer.

Avoid landing salmon with a tailer. When the noose tightens around the tail, protective film and tissue are removed, making the fish susceptible to infection.

FISHING FOR TROPHY TROUT

An average stream fisherman seldom catches a big trout. The trophy fisherman catches considerably fewer trout, but the challenge of outwitting a big one makes up for the lack of quantity. To improve his chances of taking a trophy, he fishes in different places and uses different techniques than other anglers.

Look for big trout in the deepest pools or undercuts, or at least in areas where they can easily reach a deep-water retreat. Just how deep is relative. In a small creek, a 4-foot (1.2 m) pool is deep enough to hold a big one. In a large river, an 8-foot (2.4 m) pool may not be deep enough.

Big trout prey on smaller ones, so when a likely looking pool fails to produce even a small trout, this may be a clue that the pool is home to an exceptionally large trout. It pays to try such a pool from time to time rather than giving up on it.

Of course, some streams are more likely to produce big trout than others. Tailwater streams, coastal streams, and streams connected to large lakes generally yield the biggest trout.

A trophy trout is more likely to be near the bottom than is a small trout, so sinking flies or deep-running lures are usually more effective than dry flies or shallow-runners.

Because fish make up a greater percentage of a trout's diet as it grows older, fish-imitating lures like minnow plugs, spinners, and streamers take larger trout than do small, insect-imitating flies. Some trophy hunters use streamers that measure up to 4 inches (10.2 cm).

Big dry flies can be deadly during a hatch of large insects. In the northern Rockies, trophy-class trout that normally ignore insects go on a feeding rampage when large stoneflies, known as salmon flies, are hatching. On many eastern streams, big trout gorge themselves during the green drake mayfly hatch.

A hefty trout does not like to exert itself too much. Rather than racing smaller trout to catch fast-moving foods, it lies in wait for the chance to grab unsuspecting prey. Regardless of the type of bait or lure, a slow presentation generally works best.

Any type of trout fishing requires an inconspicuous approach to avoid putting the fish down. However, when you're after trophies, stealth is even more important. The reason these trout have grown so large is that they have learned to sense predators, including fishermen. Some trophy specialists go to extremes to avoid detection; they cast from behind bushes, or stay upstream of the pool and let the current carry their bait to the fish. For trophy browns, serious anglers do almost all their fishing at night.

WHERE TO FIND TROPHY TROUT

Hard-to-reach pockets, like a deep hole beneath roots or branches, often hold big trout. Most anglers shy away from such spots because of snags.

Downstream reaches that would seem too warm and muddy for trout usually have high baitfish populations that attract trophy browns.

Remote stream stretches or those where brushy banks restrict access usually hold bigger trout than easily accessible stretches.

Chapter 4
FLY FISHING FOR TROUT AND SALMON

Why fly fish? After all, you can catch trout and salmon by spinning or baitcasting, both of which are easier to learn.

Fly fishing is by far the oldest of these methods, with a history stretching back centuries. So the modern fly angler, equipped with a lightweight graphite rod rather than a buggy-whip wooden pole, has the satisfaction of carrying on a long and colorful tradition.

But nostalgia, no matter how strong, can't account for the survival of this age-old method into the space age, or for the manifold increase in its popularity in recent years. Despite its ancient origins, fly fishing remains a versatile and productive way to outwit wary salmonids.

Many of the most common foods for trout can be imitated only with flies; even the tiniest spinning and casting lures are much too bulky. Aquatic insects, such as mayflies and caddisflies, make up most of the diet of stream trout. Imitations of these delicate creatures are much too light to be cast with ordinary spinning or baitcasting techniques.

In fact, flies can successfully imitate any trout food. With a 6- or 7-weight fly line and a rod to match, you can fish with anything from the tiniest midge imitations, not much bigger than a gnat, on up to streamers that simulate minnows several inches (cm) long.

The most frantic and exciting angling for stream trout comes during cloudlike insect hatches. Yet it can also be the most frustrating. The fish may be rising all around you, but if you're limited to casting hardware, you're almost certainly out of luck. When rising to a hatch, trout generally refuse all imitations of other types of food.

Some of the biggest trout feed almost entirely on baitfish. In lakes, spoons and minnow plugs usually work better for these fish than streamer flies, which don't have much action in the still water. In streams, though, the current gives streamers an erratic, undulating movement more lifelike than the steady wobbling of hardware. Generally, you can mimic the size, shape, and color of particular baitfish more closely with flies than with plugs or spoons.

Many famous trout streams have fly-fishing-only regulations. These regulations are designed to reduce hooking mortality and ensure a healthy population of trout for everyone who wants to catch fish. Even on streams that allow spinning and baitcasting equipment, such tackle makes it difficult to present a fly realistically enough for the educated trout found in these waters. For casting flies softly and maneuvering them like living creatures through a maze of current, fly fishing tackle nearly always works best.

It's true that learning to fly fish takes time and effort. To become really skilled may require several seasons of experience on the water. It's also true that you can start enjoying this traditional way of angling, and start catching fish, after only a couple brief practice sessions.

As in any other kind of fishing, the learning is part of the fun. Actually, it's a process that never ends, even if you fish a lifetime. The tips on the following pages will get you started right.

RIGGING UP

When trout are rising but won't take a fly, you may wonder if you're using the wrong pattern or perhaps the wrong size. And if you hook a fish but fail to catch it, you may ponder what mistake you made while fighting it. In both cases, however, you might be asking yourself the wrong questions.

Many costly errors in fly fishing are made even before the first cast. To present the fly realistically and to hold a running or jumping fish, you must rig your tackle carefully. It's tempting to rush the preliminaries, especially when you arrive at the stream and a hatch is already under way. Fly tackle takes longer to rig than other kinds of equipment, but experienced anglers know it's time well spent.

Do as much of the rigging as possible before you leave home. Tie a length of heavy monofilament to the tip of your fly line with a needle knot. For lines up to 4-weight, use 0.017-inch mono (0.043 cm); for 5- to 7-weight lines, 0.019-inch (0.048 cm); for 8-weight and heavier, 0.021-inch (0.053 cm). In the other end of the mono, tie a perfection loop. When finished, this mono connector should be 4 to 6 inches (10.2 to 15.2 cm) long.

Tie another perfection loop in the end of your leader butt. This loop will join to the one on the connector, making leader changes quick and simple.

Use blood knots to join a tippet to a knotless leader, and to join various sections of a knotted leader.

On the stream, thread the leader through the rod guides, and then take a minute or two to straighten it. Pull a short section repeatedly between your fingers; the stretching and heat from the friction will remove the coils. Continue until the entire leader is straight. Otherwise, it won't unroll properly on the cast, and when you fish with subsurface flies the springy mono will keep you from detecting strikes.

Instead of straightening the leader with bare fingers, you can use a leader straightener. Then you can pull harder without cutting or burning your skin.

Always check the sharpness of your hook. Try running the point across a fingernail; it will catch in the nail if well sharpened. Dull hooks should be touched up with a hone. Make sure the point hasn't been damaged by snagging on rocks. If it's bent slightly you can usually straighten it carefully with a small pair of needle-nose pliers. But if any of the point is broken off, discard the fly. Many anglers flatten the barbs

TYING LOOPS IN LEADER BUTT & MONO CONNECTOR

Perfection loop. (top to bottom) Make a loop by passing the free end under the standing line. Wrap the free end around, to form a second loop on top of the first. Wrap the free end around once more, passing it between the loops. Pass the top loop through the bottom one. Tighten and trim.

LOOP-TO-LOOP CONNECTION

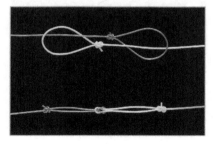

Loop connection. (top) Pass the leader-butt loop through the loop in the fly-line connector, then run all the leader through the butt loop. (bottom) Snug.

on their fly hooks for easier penetration, and for quicker removal with no injury to the fish (or fisherman).

For tying subsurface flies to your tippet, the best knot is a Duncan loop. A loop knot allows the fly to swing naturally in the current, but you can sometimes get by with a knot that draws tight on the hook eye. The Duncan loop is stronger than other loop knots, but it may tighten on the eye under the pressure of a snag or a large fish. With your fingernails, you can usually slide the knot back up the line to reopen the loop.

Tie dry flies on with a clinch knot. When tightening, make certain to center the knot at the front of the hook eye, with the line pointing straight ahead or slightly downward. This ensures the fly will float in the most natural attitude.

TYING TIPPET TO LEADER	TYING SUBSURFACE FLIES TO TIPPET	TYING DRY FLIES TO TIPPET

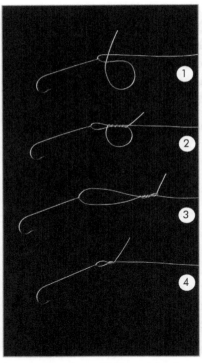

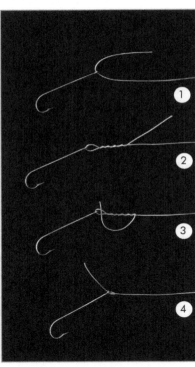

Blood knot. (1) Cross the two sections of mono. (2) With one of the ends, make four turns around the other section. (3) Bring the end back around between the two lines. (4) Repeat with the other end, inserting it in the opening so it points opposite the first end. (5) Wet the knot, then pull on the standing ends to tighten. Trim close.

Duncan loop knot. (1) Thread the tippet through the hook eye, then form a loop next to the standing line. (2) Make four to six turns around one side of the loop and the standing line. Wet the knot and (3) tighten it by pulling on the fly and the free end, then on the fly and the standing line. (4) Slide the tightened knot within 1/8 to 1/4 inch (0.32 to 0.64 cm) of the hook eye, and pull hard on the free end with needle-nose pliers to secure it there. Trim.

Double clinch knot. (1) Pass end of tippet through hook eye. (2) Wind tag end around standing line 3 1/4 to 8 times, depending on tippet diameter. (3) Bring tag end back through loop nearest hook eye. (4) Pull standing line until knot is snug against hook eye. Trim tag.

CASTING A FLY

Fly casting differs from other methods of casting in several important respects:

- Because a fly weighs so little, you cast the weight of the fly line itself, which is thicker and heavier than other kinds of line.

- Each casting stroke, forward or back, consists of two movements blended together. Using your forearm, you load the rod, raising the tip to start the line moving and to put a deep bend in the rod. You finish the stroke with a wrist snap, with a sudden application of force as in spinning. The keys to smooth fly casting are the proper timing and gradual acceleration of each stroke, not a sudden application of force as in spinning.

Gradual acceleration ensures that the line will flow out straight on the cast. If you apply too much power too soon, the rod tip will bounce at the end of the stroke, throwing waves of slack into the line. On the following stroke, this slack will make it impossible to load the rod.

The loop formed in your line as it travels forward or rearward should be narrow, no more than 2 feet (60 cm) in width. A narrow loop has little air resistance, so your line travels fast without sagging to the water, and has less chance of blowing off target.

Before attempting to fish, spend some time practicing on water or an open lawn. Any balanced trout outfit will do, but a 6-weight rod with a weight-forward floating line is ideal. Tie on a leader 7½ feet (2.3 m) long and a piece of bright yarn to simulate the fly.

Start by learning the basic overhead cast. Once you have it mastered, practice false casting, shooting line, and roll casting. Then you'll be ready to catch trout. The double haul is an advanced technique for distance casting, which you can learn later on. Usually, the most effective range for trout is just 25 to 40 feet (7.6 to 12.2 m).

HOW TO MAKE THE BASIC OVERHEAD CAST

Begin by letting out the desired amount of line in front of you. Stand facing the target with your feet spread comfortably apart. Position your rod hand so the tip of the rod is pointing in the direction of your target, with your rod, forearm, and wrist aligned. Lower your rod tip and remove the slack from the line.

Raise your rod and begin to accelerate slowly and continuously until the entire fly line is off the water.

Apply a short backward speed stroke, forcing a bend in the rod and generating the energy necessary to propel the line into the back cast.

Stop the rod crisply. A loop will form in the line as it moves overhead. The shorter the speed stroke and straighter the casting plane, the tighter the loop will be.

Pause as the back cast unrolls behind you. When the line unrolls to only a small "J" in the air, begin your forward acceleration. Apply a short forward speed stroke and immediately stop the rod. Aim your cast about eye level above your target. Let the line settle to the water while lowering the rod tip to the fishing position.

False Casting

The false cast is a necessary supplement to the basic overhead cast. Instead of letting your line and fly settle to the water on the forward cast, you keep them in the air and make another back cast. False casting serves several purposes:

- You can cancel an off-target cast; just pull into a back cast and correct your aim on the next cast forward.

- You can change directions from one cast to the next. It's difficult to pick your line off the water, make a single back cast, and aim the forward cast at a target off to your side. Instead, you false cast once in an intermediate direction and then hit the target on the next cast.

- In fishing with dry flies, a succession of false casts helps air-dry the hackle so the fly floats high and keeps its natural appearance.

- For additional distance, shoot line on a false cast. Generally, the more line you strip in on the retrieve, the more false casts it will take to cast the same distance again.

HOW TO FALSE CAST

Lift line off water as you would on a normal overhead cast.

Let the back cast unroll behind you until the line forms a small "J."

Aim your forward cast higher than you would on an overhead cast. Do not allow the line to settle on the water. Instead, wait until the small "J" forms in the line and begin another back cast. Repeat as necessary.

Shooting Line

Usually you want to cast more line than you pick up from the water. If your previous cast was 40 feet (12.2 m) long and you retrieved 15 feet (4.6 m) while fishing the fly, you need to shoot line if you want to reach out more than the 25 feet (7.6 m) you picked up. To do so, you simply release line while the loop is in the air; the unrolling line pulls more out behind it.

Before starting a cast, make sure you have enough running line stripped off the reel. Let it lie on the water, or hold it in loose coils with your line hand. You can shoot line on a forward cast (shown below) or on a back cast.

Shoot line by forming a large "O" with your thumb and forefinger immediately after the wrist snap on the cast. Allow loose line to flow, or shoot, through it.

How to Roll Cast

When obstructions prevent a normal back cast, use the roll cast. With this technique you cannot reach out as far as with a normal cast; the maximum distance is about 40 feet (12.2 m). Roll casting must be practiced on water, not land. A double-taper line works best; with a weight-forward, the running line is too light to pick up the belly.

Ease your rod tip rearward and tilt it away from you, so the line hangs outside the rod and slightly behind it. Then pause until the line stops moving.

Move your arm forward and downward smoothly, then accelerate quickly and make a forward speed stroke, and stop the rod crisply. The line will roll toward the target in a wide loop and straighten.

The Double Haul

Long casts are often necessary in salmon and steelhead fishing, and occasionally in other types of trout fishing. The double haul increases line speed on the back cast and again on the forward cast, so you can make long casts and punch into the wind. This technique can increase your casting distance by 50 percent.

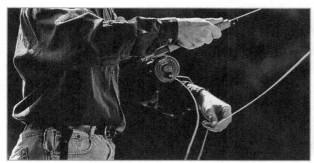

Make a short, smooth downward tug, or haul, about 4 to 6 inches (10 to 15 cm), during the acceleration phase of the back cast.

Bring your hand back up immediately after the haul. Let the line unroll behind you as you would on a normal overhead cast.

Make a second haul, equal in length to the first, during the acceleration phase of the forward cast.

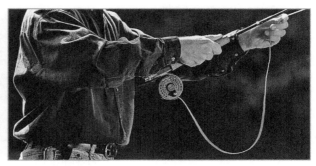

Bring your line hand back up immediately after the haul. If you are shooting line, form an "O" with the fingers of your line hand instead.

COMMON MISTAKES IN FLY CASTING

Starting the back cast with the rod pointed high allows slack line to sag from the rod tip. With the slack, you cannot fully load the rod.

Turning the arm or wrist so the reel aims outward waves the rod in a semicircle, widening line loops. The rod must go straight back and forward.

FISHING WITH DRY FLIES

Nothing is more suspenseful than watching a big trout or salmon rise slowly to a floating fly, perhaps to reject it at the last moment, or perhaps to engulf it and give you a battle demanding all your finesse.

Despite the intimidating technical discussions in books and magazines, dry-fly angling is generally the easiest way to fool a trout with a fly. It offers these advantages:

• You can read surface currents easily.

• If the trout are rising, you can see where they are and often what they're feeding on.

• You know exactly where your fly is and whether it's working as it should.

• You can detect strikes by sight.

Dry flies are designed to imitate the adult stages of various aquatic insects. The classic dry, with a stiff tail and hackle and a pair of upright wings, is a good approximation of a mayfly. Stonefly imitations are similar but larger, with a single hair wing angled backward. Caddis patterns are small, like mayfly imitations, but have wings lying tentlike along the body; they are sometimes tied without hackle. Midge flies, almost microscopic, have hackle but no wings.

When selecting a dry fly on the stream, most anglers attempt to match the hatch. Recognize, however, that trout often feed selectively, and the particular insects you notice first, the biggest or most abundant species, may not be the ones they want. Examine the rises and the naturals adrift on the stream to determine what the fish actually are taking. If you don't have a fly that duplicates them in size, shape, and color, settle for matching just the size. An artificial slightly smaller than the real thing usually works better than one that's bigger.

Traditionally, dry-fly anglers have fished in an upstream direction. The fly drifts toward you, so you strip in line and can easily pick up the short length remaining on the water when you're ready for the next cast. Cast diagonally upstream, rather than straight up, so your leader and line won't drift over the fish and spook it. To reach difficult lies, you may want to cast across stream or downstream.

Regardless of the direction you cast, always drop your fly well upstream of the fish and let it drift into position. Remember, the rises of a fish are misleading; they do not indicate the spot where the trout actually lies.

On a drift, you must avoid drag. If the current pulls your line so the fly is dragged across the surface, the trout will refuse it and may even stop rising. Keep some slack in your leader at all times, and in your line, if needed. Once the line is on the water, you can mend it to maintain slack. When you fish in a downstream direction, simply pay out your line as fast as the current takes it.

At times, the drag-free drift may be less productive than skating a dry fly across the surface. You do this by making a short cast downstream, then holding your rod tip high and shaking it gently from side to side while stripping in line. The fly will skip erratically on the water, like a caddisfly attempting flight. The action is very different from the steady slide across the surface resulting from drag.

Dry flies often catch trout and salmon when they aren't rising, and even when no insects are hatching at all. Under these conditions, you drift your fly naturally to the spots where fish are most likely to lie, or skate it over them. An effective tactic is to make several casts to a single spot, creating the illusion of a hatch.

Dry flies are used in sizes 8 to 28 for most trout, and sizes 2 to 8 for steelhead and Atlantic salmon.

How to Fish Across Stream with the Reach Cast

This cast puts a wide upstream curve of slack in your line, doubling the length of your drift before a downstream curve, or belly, forms in the line and drag sets in. You can make a backhand reach cast (shown) or a forehand, depending on the direction of the current.

Make a normal forward cast, allowing some line to shoot through the guides as the loop starts to unroll toward the target.

Point your rod tip as far as possible to the side from which the current is flowing. Continue to shoot line while moving your rod to the side.

Stop the line when your fly is over the target. The line falls well upstream of the fly, so you won't have to mend so soon.

How to Fish Downstream with the S-Cast

When you fish downstream, the S-cast will put slack in your entire line, giving you a long drag-free drift. A lot of narrow S-curves work better than a few wide ones; wide curves reduce casting accuracy and are difficult to pick up from the water when you set the hook.

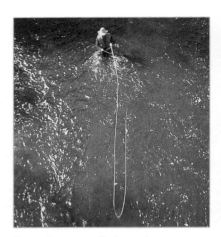

Direct the cast well above the water, shooting line. Use just enough power to reach the target, so you don't have to brake the cast.

Shake the rod rapidly from side to side, forming curves in the line. The line must continue to shoot, or the curves will straighten.

Bring the rod tip down as the line settles. The fly will drift freely until the curves wash out. You can extend the drift by paying out line.

FISHING WITH WET FLIES

The standard wet fly has almost become a museum piece. A century ago, it was the only artificial fly in use in America; today the angler who wants a sunken fly is far more likely to tie on a streamer or nymph, which more closely resembles important trout food such as baitfish and larval insects.

Traditional wet-fly techniques are the simplest and most effortless in fly fishing. There's less casting than with dry flies, so you cover the water more quickly. Also, wets are effective in fast, broken currents that would quickly drown any dry. Wet flies are generally much smaller and less air-resistant than streamers, so they're easier to cast. In addition, your presentation and retrieve need not be as precise as in fishing with nymphs.

Wet flies have soft, absorbent hackle for quick sinking and lifelike action. The standard wet has a feather wing; dull-tinted patterns of this type are thought to represent drowned adult insects. Feather-wing wets with gaudy colors and metallic tinsels may suggest tiny baitfish, but serve mainly as attractors useful for brook trout and Atlantic salmon. Some wet patterns, called hackle flies, lack wings; these may resemble insect larvae or leeches.

The most popular wet flies today are specialized types. Large patterns with wings of hair or marabou, often in bright attractor colors, are commonly used for steelhead and salmon. Fat-bodied hackle flies called wooly worms, which have hackle along their entire length, are favorites for trout of all kinds on big western rivers.

Wet flies are often drifted at random, covering lots of potential holding water rather than particular lies. The wet-fly drift technique, with a floating or sink tip line, works especially well in long runs and riffles that lack large boulders or other obvious cover. In such places, trout take shelter near small obstructions or in depressions in the bottom that may be invisible from the surface.

You can also fish specific targets. Cast across the stream and let your fly drift into the calm pockets around logs, rocks, and other objects. When it reaches a pocket, feed line into the current—the fly stays where it is, but the belly expands downstream. Otherwise, the current would sweep the fly away immediately.

In fall and winter steelheading, it's usually necessary to fish wet flies very deep. Use the wet-fly drift with a fast-sinking shooting head or a lead-core head. Many wet flies designed for steelhead have weighted bodies or bead heads; they will bounce along the bottom without snagging if the rocks are rounded.

Wet flies are used in sizes 10 to 18 for most trout, and sizes 2 to 8 for steelhead and salmon.

HOW TO FISH WITH THE WET-FLY DRIFT

Make a short cast across the current. In swift water, cast slightly downstream to minimize the belly and keep the line from being pulled downstream too quickly. In slower current, cast slightly upstream, so more belly will form and speed up the fly.

Mend your line to control the speed of your fly. If the fly swings too slowly, make a downstream mend (shown) to increase belly and accelerate the fly. If your fly swings too quickly, throw an upstream mend to reduce the belly and slow the fly.

Let the fly swing until it hangs in the current below you and begins to rise. You'll get a high percentage of your strikes at this point.

Lengthen each subsequent cast by 1 to 3 feet (0.3 to 0.9 m) until you've covered all the water you can reach. Then, take a step or two downstream and repeat the process.

FISHING WITH NYMPHS

Day in and day out, the odds favor the fly fisherman who uses a nymph. No matter how low or high the stream may be, no matter how cold or warm the weather, the naturals that nymphs imitate are always present and available to the trout.

Nymphs are intended to copy the immature forms of aquatic insects, including mayflies, stoneflies, caddisflies, dragonflies, damselflies, and midges. Some nymphs are close imitations of particular species, as exact as fly tiers can make them. Others are impressionistic, meant to suggest a variety of naturals in form, size, and coloration. Many nymphs of both these types have bodies that are thick at the front and thinner at the rear, simulating the wing pads and abdomens of the real thing. Usually, there's a soft, sparse hackle to serve as legs.

A nymph pattern may be tied in weighted and unweighted versions. Weighted nymphs have lead or copper wire wound onto the hook shank under the body material. They are used for fishing near the bottom, especially in fast currents. Unweighted nymphs work well for fishing shallow; because they have livelier action, many experts prefer them for fishing deep in slow water as well. To carry them deep, attach split shot or lead wrap to the leader. A few nymphs are designed to float, imitating the immature insect at the moment it arrives on the surface to transform into an adult.

No one becomes a complete nymph fisherman overnight. Techniques for fishing nymphs are far more numerous and varied than those for any other type of fly. Some are simple, but others are the most challenging of all ways of catching trout.

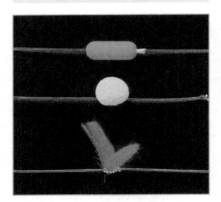

Popular strike indicators include: (top to bottom) Styrofoam float pegged in place with a toothpick; Adhesive foam, which pinches onto your leader and sticks in place; and Colored yarn tied into a blood knot in your leader.

Depending on species and stage of life, the naturals may crawl across the bottom, burrow in it, swim, or simply tumble along with the current. Thus, the nymph fisherman can work his fly realistically by drifting it freely with the current, or by twitching or stripping it along at various depths.

Detecting strikes in nymph fishing can be difficult. When you use a natural drift, it's generally impossible to feel the hit. The best solution is to use a floating line with a bright-colored tip, a leader with a fluorescent butt, or some kind of strike indicator (see photo) attached to the leader. If you see any twitch or hesitation, set the hook.

For greatest sensitivity, strike indicators should be positioned as close to the fly as possible. To fish shallow, place the indicator just above the tippet knot. To fish deep, move it back toward the leader butt.

Keep your casts short so you can see the twitch more clearly. If you use a sink tip line, keep an eye on the point where the lighter-colored floating portion appears below the surface.

One of the easiest nymph techniques, and one of the most effective, is the wet-fly drift. It's a good way to fish runs and riffles that lack obvious cover to cast to. By planning a drift carefully, you can also use this technique to swing your fly close to boulders or logs, or to nymphing trout you can actually see.

Sometimes these nymphing fish are visible only as flashes near the streambed, as they turn and dart in the current to feed. At other times, their tails make swirls on the surface when they tip nose down to take nymphs on the bottom, or their backs may break water when they feed on naturals that are only a few inches deep. Anglers often mistake these swirls for rises to adult insects, and make futile attempts to catch the trout with dry flies.

When drifting a nymph to a feeding fish, try to sink it exactly to the fish's eye level. To increase the depth of a drift, angle your cast farther upstream so the fly will have more time to sink before reaching the trout. Use a weighted nymph if necessary, or add a suitable amount of weight to your leader.

In the still water of pools, try making a long cast, letting the nymph sink near the bottom, then retrieving it in short twitches. In very cold water, especially in the early season, a nymph allowed to lie motionless on the bottom and twitched only occasionally may be more effective than anything else except live bait. Stay alert for strikes; a trout may pick up the loitering nymph and drop it instantly.

Nymphs used for trout range from size 1/0 to 18.

HOW TO FISH A NYMPH UPSTREAM

Make a short cast upstream, so your nymph will drift to a visible fish or probable lie. If possible, cast at an angle rather than straight upstream, so your line won't drift over the fish and spook it.

Strip line in as the current carries the nymph toward you. Let the fly drift naturally; to prevent drag, your line should have slight curves of slack. Twitch the fly when it reaches the fish or the lie.

Watch your strike indicator closely. If it flicks or pauses at any time during the drift, set the hook instantly. Too long a delay, or too much slack in the drifting line, will cause you to miss the strike.

HOW TO FISH A CURRENT EDGE WITH A DOWNSTREAM MEND

Angle your cast upstream into the edge of a fast current. Trout will hold in the slower water near shore, watching for nymphs to wash down in the fast current, and darting out to grab them.

Mend your line by flipping a curve of slack downstream. Because the tip of the line is in the faster water, a belly forms upstream, the reverse of the usual situation. Without a mend, the fly would drift slower than the current.

FISHING WITH STREAMERS

If you're serious about catching big trout, try fishing with streamers. The real heavyweights feed almost exclusively on baitfish; most streamers are tied to mimic shiners, dace, sculpins, chubs, darters, and even young trout.

Not that streamers are invariably the flies to select. When the water conditions are ideal for feeding, trout show more interest in dries, nymphs, and wets. Streamers produce most dependably when dries and wets don't, such as during periods when the water is very cold or discolored.

Pick the right times, and you may come up with a trophy. Not only do streamers attract the attention of big trout better than small flies, they also give you a better chance of hanging on once a fish is hooked. The big, stout hooks hold securely, and the heavy tippets generally used with streamers make break-offs less likely.

The traditional streamer has a wing of long hackle feathers, but other types are more popular today. Patterns with hair wings are often called bucktails, even if the hair is synthetic or comes from animals other than deer. Another type, the Zonker, has a strip of soft fur tied along the top of the hook. Muddlers have large heads, usually of clipped deer hair, to simulate the outline of sculpins.

Some brightly colored streamers do not closely imitate any baitfish, but instead work as attractors. Often, these bright flies draw more strikes than realistic ones. Or, trout may swirl at an attractor pattern, revealing their whereabouts, but refuse to take it. Then you can switch to a realistic streamer or some other type of fly more likely to draw a strike.

Because of their size and bulk, streamers produce more vibration than other flies when stripped through the water. This extra attraction helps fish locate them in roily water or after dark. Muddler and diver patterns, with their oversize heads, make the most underwater disturbance.

Like nymphs, streamers are tied with or without built-in weight, and may be fished with floating or sink tip lines, or with sinking shooting heads. Split shot or other weight may be added to the leader as needed.

The wet-fly drift is a good basic technique for streamers. You can twitch the fly during the drift for a more convincing minnow-like action. Mend the line often, so the fly does not speed unnaturally through the current. Proper mending also keeps the streamer drifting broadside to the current, so it's more visible to fish lying in wait.

In slower current that does not give the fly much action, you can cast across stream, then strip the fly back toward you as it slowly swings downstream. No mending is needed, since the fly is retrieved before a wide belly can develop. The streamer simulates a baitfish darting across the current. Even when conditions are not ideal for streamers, this technique enables you to cover water very quickly, tempting trout to swirl at the fly as they would at an attractor pattern.

Streamers are used in sizes 1/0 to 10 for trout, sizes 1/0 to 4 for salmon.

HOW TO FISH A MUDDLER ON THE SURFACE

Twitch a muddler across flat water, pausing occasionally, to imitate a grasshopper or struggling baitfish. Work the fly close to grassy banks, especially near undercuts. The head and hair collar behind it should be dressed with floatant.

HOW TO HANG A STREAMER IN THE CURRENT

Swing your streamer near a boulder or log. Let it hang there a minute or so, waving in the current; twitch it occasionally. This works well for steelhead and salmon, which often strike only if given a long look at the fly.

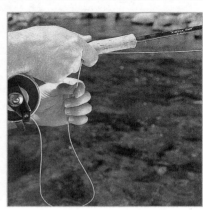

Keep a foot (30 cm) of slack line between the reel and your finger when hanging a streamer in current. On a strike, you can instantly release this slack to soften the shock to the tippet.

FISHING WITH SPECIAL PURPOSE FLIES

Historically, almost all flies were tied to imitate insects or baitfish. However, anglers have come to realize that fish aren't always interested in such offerings. At times, other foods are more abundant and the trout prefer them to the everyday fare.

Certain of these morsels, such as leeches, crayfish, and salmon eggs, seem to defy imitation with fur and feathers. Still, imaginative fly tiers have come up with realistic copies, and inventive anglers have devised techniques to bring them to life.

The most popular of these special purpose flies are terrestrials. These simulate land insects such as ants, grasshoppers, crickets, beetles, and inchworms, any of which may fall onto the water. Terrestrial flies are effective throughout the warm months. They're especially useful in late summer, when aquatic hatches wane. Terrestrials are fished on the surface in slow to moderate current, where the surface is relatively smooth.

Ant imitations often work better than standard dry flies on days when no trout are rising. Floating ants in sizes 18 to 22 are drifted close to the banks, where natural ants are most likely to be. These tiny flies are difficult to see, so keep your casts short, and strike gently at any rise near your fly. Sinking ants are usually tied in sizes 8 to 20. Drift ant imitations with a floating line, mending often to avoid drag.

Grasshopper patterns, in sizes 4 to 14, are most productive in meadow streams, particularly on windy days when the naturals are blown onto the water. Dead drift them along grassy banks, adding an occasional twitch. Beetles and jassids (small flat-bodied insects, also known as leafhoppers) are inconspicuous on the water, but in warm weather the trout may feed on them selectively. Beetle imitations are tied in sizes 10 to 20; jassids, sizes 16 to 22. A dead drift on the surface works best.

Leech flies are among the top lures for big trout. These are big flies, size 2 to 10. The dressings, in most cases, consist mainly of marabou or rabbit fur. These soft materials have an undulating action that matches the squirming of the naturals. Work leech flies in slow current with the wet-fly drift, twitching them from time to time. In still water, retrieve with long, slow strips; a jerky action would make the fur or marabou flare out from the hook, spoiling the illusion of a real leech.

It's not unusual in spring creeks to catch a trout that's gorged on tiny crustaceans, called scuds.

Scud patterns imitate tiny crustaceans that are superabundant in many trout streams, especially spring creeks. Trout often gorge themselves on scuds, burrowing into weedbeds and rooting them out. It's not unusual to catch a trout that is so stuffed with scuds that it regurgitates them when you attempt to unhook it. When trout gorge themselves this heavily, they're tough to catch, but you may be able to draw a strike by drifting a scud pattern so it nearly hits the fish on the nose. Scud flies range from size 10 to 20.

Crayfish flies should be worked close to rocky streambeds, either drifting them with the current or stripping them briskly through quiet water. Crayfish are most plentiful in limestone streams, and become most active in low light. A good time to fish the imitations, in sizes 1/0 to 8, is at dusk or after dark.

In streams with runs of Pacific salmon, other salmonids like rainbows, Dolly Varden, and grayling feed heavily on salmon eggs. Fly anglers take trophy fish by dead-drifting egg flies in fluorescent red, pink, or orange. Use just enough weight on your leader to reach bottom; big trout may drop the fly immediately if they feel resistance. Egg patterns also are tied in white and chartreuse to imitate the spawn of suckers and other fishes.

Chapter 5

SPINNING AND BAITCASTING TECHNIQUES

For the average fisherman, spinning and baitcasting are much easier than fly fishing. Plus, in some situations, they catch more and bigger trout. Because trout eat more baitfish and fewer insects as they grow larger, good-sized baits and lures have more appeal than small flies.

The monofilament line used with spinning and baitcasting gear offers several advantages to stream fishermen. The small diameter line cuts the current much better than fly line, so drag is not as much of a problem, and you can fish deep more easily. Mono is also less wind-resistant, which makes casting in a headwind or crosswind considerably easier. Fly line is highly visible; if you cast over a trout, or allow your line to drift ahead of the fly, the fish may spook. With mono, your presentation need not be as precise.

When heavy rains cloud a stream, fly fishing may be tough, but spinfishermen and baitcasters continue catching trout. The fish can still detect the scent of natural bait or the sound and vibration of plugs and spinners.

On a narrow, brushy stream, fly casting is almost impossible because streamside obstacles foul your back cast. But with a short, ultralight spinning outfit, you can flip small lures beneath overhanging branches and into fish pockets that otherwise would be difficult to reach. Spinning gear is also an advantage on wide streams because you can make long casts and cover a lot of water in a hurry.

Baitcasting gear is the best choice for exceptionally large trout and salmon. The level-wind reel eliminates the line twist problems that plague spinfishermen when big fish strip line from their reels.

JIG FISHING

Until recently, jigs were reserved for warmwater species like bass and walleyes. Few anglers even considered using them for trout. Yet jigs do have a place in trout fishing, and in the hands of an expert they can be deadly. Even fly fishermen are discovering the effectiveness of nymphs tied on tiny jig hooks.

Jigs resemble favorite trout foods such as minnows, insect larvae, crustaceans, leeches, and salmon eggs. Try to match your jig color to the fish's natural food. A black or brown jig, for instance, would be a good match for most insect larvae; an orange jig, for salmon eggs.

When trout are aggressive, a jig with a tail dressing of soft plastic, marabou, or hair is all you need. When trout are fussy, try tipping your jig with some type of natural bait, like a piece of worm or a small minnow.

Jigs work as well for small trout as for larger trout and salmon. They cast easily and sink rapidly in the current. A jig of the proper weight hugs the bottom and is not swept by the current as much as most other lures. And, jigs are versatile: You can drift them downstream, retrieve them across stream, or jig them vertically.

DOWNSTREAM DRIFTING. To catch trout feeding in riffles, cast a 1/32- to 1/80-ounce (0.89 to 0.35 g) microjig upstream, then let it drift down through the riffle. Keep your rod tip high, reeling up slack as the jig drifts. Strikes may be hard to detect, but you can attach a strike indicator (inset photo below), just as you would in nymph fishing.

For casting these tiny jigs, use a 4½- to 5½-foot (1.4 to 1.7 m) ultralight spinning rod with a slow to medium action. Spool your reel with limp, 2- to 4-pound (0.9 to 1.8 kg) mono.

CROSS-STREAM RETRIEVE. In deeper water, use a heavier jig, $\frac{1}{16}$ to 1/4 ounce (1.8 to 7.1 g). Quarter your cast upstream, aiming for targets like boulders and logs. Let the jig sink to the bottom, then retrieve it in a series of short twitches, lowering the jig back to the bottom with a taut line after each twitch. If the bottom-bouncing technique doesn't pay off, try a twitching retrieve in the mid-depths and just beneath the surface. Sometimes a faster retrieve will trigger a strike.

With these heavier jigs, use a medium-power, fast-action spinning rod, from 5¼ to 6 feet (1.6 to 1.8 m) in length, with limp 4- to 8-pound (1.8 to 3.6 kg) mono.

VERTICAL JIGGING. This technique works well for salmon and large trout in deep pools and runs of good-sized rivers. Simply lower a jig or jigging spoon to the bottom, then jig vertically as the boat drifts downstream. Keep your line taut as the lure sinks; set the hook at the slightest tug. Use a lure weighing from 3/8 ounce to 2 ounces (10.6 to 56.7 g), depending on current speed and water depth.

A heavy baitcasting outfit works best for vertical jigging. Use a 5 ½- to 6-foot (1.7 to 1.8 m), fast-action rod with 12- to 20-pound (5.5 to 9.1 kg) mono. For salmon, you may need mono up to 30-pound (13.6 kg) test.

CASTING WITH HARDWARE

The term "hardware" means all hard-bodied lures like spoons, spinners, and plugs. Hardware attracts trout by flash and vibration. By casting with hardware, you can cover a lot of water in a hurry. The technique works best from later spring through early fall, when higher water temperatures make trout more aggressive.

Compared to most other trout fishing techniques, hardware fishing is easy. Simply cast across stream, then regulate the speed of your retrieve so the lure ticks the bottom. When trout are actively feeding, ticking the bottom may not be necessary; the fish will swim upward to grab the lure.

Exactly how you angle your cast depends on the lure, the water depth, and the current speed. The more you angle it upstream, the deeper the lure will run. If the lure is bouncing on the bottom too much, angle the cast farther downstream. This way, water resistance from the current will keep the lure off the bottom.

Standard spinners and thin spoons are popular in small streams, where distance casting is not important.

Sonic spinners, which have a shaft that passes through the blade, are extremely popular in the West. The blade starts turning at the very low retrieve speed.

Weight-forward spinners and medium to thick spoons are a better choice in bigger rivers, or in those with deep water or fast current. These heavier lures can be cast much farther, and they run deeper.

Floating minnow plugs work well in small streams, but sinking minnow plugs and diving crankbaits are more effective in deeper current. With spinners, spoons, and sinking minnow plugs, the slower you retrieve, the deeper the lures will run. Floating minnow plugs and crankbaits run deepest with a medium to medium-fast retrieve.

For casting spinners, small spoons, and minnow plugs, use a 5- to 6-foot (1.5 to 1.8 m) light spinning outfit with 2- to 6-pound (0.9 to 2.7 kg) mono; for larger spoons and diving plugs, use a 5 ½- to 7-foot (1.7 to 2.1 m) medium-power spinning outfit with 6- to 8-pound (2.7 to 3.6 kg) mono.

Steelhead and salmon fishermen often use 8- to 9-foot (2.4 to 2.7 m) medium- to heavy-power spinning rods with 8- to 17-pound (3.6 to 7.7 kg) mono.

To avoid line twist, attach spinners and spoons with a small ball-bearing snap-swivel. Or, splice in a swivel about 6 inches (15.2 cm) ahead of the lure. Attach minnow plugs with a small snap or a Duncan loop knot; attach crankbaits with a snap or a double clinch knot.

Crank a floating minnow plug through a riffle in early morning or late evening to catch feeding trout. From a downstream position, cast to the head of the riffle, then reel rapidly through the riffle and the downstream run. After a few casts, move to the next riffle.

Hang your lure in the current to fish hard-to-reach pockets such as holes beneath log jams, brush piles, overhanging limbs, or undercut banks. From an upstream position, cast just short of the pocket, let out a little line, then allow the current to work your lure.

Work the cover farthest downstream and closest to you first. Then, a hooked fish will not spook others in unfished water when the current sweeps it downstream, or in unfished water close to you when you reel it in.

TROLLING

When you troll, your lure is in the water all the time, maximizing your chances of catching fish. Trolling offers several other advantages over casting: It's an easier technique for the novice; it enables you to cover more water; and where multiple lines are legal, you can troll with several lures at once.

Trolling works best in big rivers that have long stretches of deep water with slow to moderate current. It's not well-suited to river stretches with lots of riffles or rapids, and not recommended for shallow or very clear water. Because the boat passes over the fish before the lure arrives, spooking may be a big problem. You can reduce spooking by trolling in S-curves. This way the lure does not track continuously in the boat's wake.

Another way to avoid spooking fish is to troll with side planers (photo above). These devices attach to your line, pulling it well to the side of the boat's wake. They also let you cover a wider swath of water. Another way to fish side planers is to walk along shore, using the planer to carry your line to midstream waters you couldn't reach by casting.

Diving planes also attach to your line, taking the lure deep. The unweighted type is all you need in most streams; weighted ones generally run too deep.

You can troll for practically any salmonid, but the technique is used most often for anadromous fishes like steelhead and Pacific salmon.

Baitcasting gear works best for trolling. A good trolling rod is 7 to 9 feet (2.1 to 2.7 m) long, stiff enough to handle the water resistance against the lure, but light enough at the tip to telegraph the lure's action. Use abrasion-resistant mono, from 6- to 20-pound (2.7 to 9.1 kg) test depending on the size of the fish. A depth finder helps you follow breaks in the bottom contour.

Most anglers troll with deep-diving crankbaits. You can also use minnow plugs, spoons, jigs, and spinner-and-bait combinations. It's a good idea to keep your lures near the bottom, except when trout are feeding on insects or salmon smolts, and will come up for a lure. Pacific salmon and steelhead feed very little in streams, but may strike a deep-running crankbait out of irritation or in defense of their territory. Normally, no extra weight is needed to get a crankbait to the bottom, but you may have to add weight to other lures.

Trolling styles used in stream fishing for trout and salmon include slipping, upstream trolling, and downstream trolling.

SLIPPING. The term "slipping" means letting the boat drift slowly downstream, reducing its speed with a motor or oars while allowing the lures to trail in the current. As long as the boat drifts more slowly than the current, the force of the water will give the lures action. Some trout fishermen refer to this technique as "backtrolling."

To cover wide channels, zigzag your boat while slipping. This allows you to cover more water on the drift, a big adventure if you don't have a motor. It also gives your lures more action, causing them to speed up and slow down, rise and fall.

Slipping is effective year-round, but works especially well in cold water; the slow-moving lure appeals to lethargic fish. The technique has one major advantage over other trolling methods: The lure passes over the fish before the boat does, so they're less likely to spook.

UPSTREAM TROLLING. You can troll upstream only in slow current. Otherwise, water resistance is so great that the lure is forced to the surface. Where the current is slow enough you can troll upstream, then turn around and troll back down, keeping your lures in the water.

DOWNSTREAM TROLLING. This technique is often used to present spinners or other lures that do not require much current for good action. Trolling downstream slightly faster than the current gives these lures enough action, yet they look like drifting food. To troll slowly enough, you may have to shift your motor between forward and neutral every few seconds. When using lures like spoons and crankbaits, you will have to troll somewhat faster.

By trolling downstream, you are in a better position to fight the fish. The current pushes a hooked fish in the direction the boat moves, reducing the possibility of breaking the line or tearing out the hooks.

SPINFISHING WITH FLIES

Even if you don't own a fly rod, you can fly fish with spinning gear. In fact, spinning with flies works better than fly fishing in some situations. In deep water, for instance, you can attach split shot to mono line and reach bottom more easily than with fly line. Also, in high winds, mono is easier to control.

In streams with flies-only regulations, spinning gear is usually legal, as long as the lure is a fly. However, to cast the fly you must attach some extra weight.

With a sinking fly, simply add a split shot or two about a foot (30 cm) up the line. Leader wrap, lead sleeves, or a good-sized strike indicator will also add weight. Strike indicators help detect light pickups as well.

Dry flies and sinking flies can be rigged with a weighted float or a plastic bubble, which can be partially filled with water for extra casting weight. If you use a clear float or bubble, trout will pay little attention to it. Then again, a float or bubble splashing down close to a fish, or drifting over it ahead of the fly, may cause it to spook.

A long, soft rod is best for casting flies and manipulating them in the water. A stiff rod doesn't flex enough to cast a light weight, and could snap a light leader when you set the hook. A 6½- to 7½-foot (1.9 to 2.3 m), slow-action spinning rod, or an 8½- to 9½-foot (2.6 to 2.9 m), 4- to 6-weight fly rod with a spinning reel is a good choice. Spool your reel with 2- to 8-pound (0.9 to 3.6 kg), limp mono.

Many spinfishermen use line that is too heavy, and add too much weight, inhibiting the movement of the fly. Always use the lightest line practical for the conditions, and the lightest weight that will allow you to cast and reach the desired depth. Too much weight causes snagging problems; and even with minimal weight, strikes are more difficult to detect than with fly-fishing gear.

OTHER RIGS FOR SPINFISHING WITH FLIES

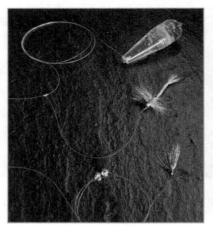

Make a dropper rig (top) by tying a blood knot 2 feet (0.6 m) up your line, leaving a 1-foot (0.3 m) tag end. Tie a float or bubble to the line, a dry fly or terrestrial to the dropper. Make a split shot rig (bottom) by pinching shot 6 to 12 inches (15.2 to 30.5 cm) above the fly.

HOW TO FISH A DROPPER RIG

Quarter your cast upstream above a rise, then raise your rod so the fly just reaches the water. Drift the fly over the rise, making sure you keep the float out of the fish's window. Occasionally lift the rod to dabble the fly on the surface.

TIPS FOR SPINFISHING WITH FLIES

Use a leader sleeve instead of split shot when fishing on a snaggy bottom. The cylindrical sleeve slips along the bottom better than a round split shot. Slide the sleeve onto your line, then tie on a leader; the knot acts as a stop.

Tie a wet-fly/dry-fly rig for use with a plastic bubble. Make a dropper by tying a blood knot, leaving a 3-inch (7.6 cm) tag end. Tie a dry fly to the dropper; it doubles as a strike indicator. Tie a wet fly to the end of the line.

NATURAL BAIT

Fly fishermen frown on the idea of using spoons, spinners, and other hardware to catch trout, and the idea of using natural bait is even farther down their list of tolerable tactics. Still, there's no denying that natural bait catches lots of trout, and it's often the method of choice for introducing children to the sport. If you wish to use natural bait, read the local fishing regulations carefully to make certain it's permitted on the waters you're fishing.

The major drawback of natural bait is the problem of deep hooking. Even a small trout often takes the bait so deeply that it's impossible to remove the hook without causing serious injury. If you plan to release your trout, don't use live bait. If you must release a deeply hooked trout, cut the line rather than trying to remove the hook.

Another disadvantage of many natural baits is the difficulty of keeping them alive and carrying them, especially if you're wading. Also, in some states, certain natural baits, like minnows, are illegal for trout.

Trout and salmon rely on their sense of smell to a greater extent than most other gamefish. They can detect dissolved substances in minute concentrations, as evidenced by the ability of sea-run salmon and steelhead to return to their home stream on the basis of its unique odor. So it's not surprising that they use their remarkable sense of smell to help them find food.

Natural bait appeals to this highly developed sense. Smell is especially important during periods of high, muddy water. Under these conditions, trout cannot see flies or hardware, but they can easily detect the odor of natural bait.

Push a size 6 or 8 hook through the broken end of a half crawler (top), or through the middle whole crawler (bottom) Or, hook the crawler two or three times, like a garden worm.

In early spring, when the water is still cold and few insects are hatching, natural bait usually outproduces flies by a wide margin. Natural bait is also a good choice in streams that do not have many insects. In addition, big trout or those in heavily fished streams can be extremely wary, closely inspecting any potential food item. They're likely to recognize any imitation as a fake.

Bait fishermen often make the mistake of using heavy line and a big hook, then adding a heavy sinker and a golf ball-sized bobber. This type of rig will seldom catch a trout. For most stream trout, bait-fishing specialists use light spinning tackle with 2- to 4-pound (0.9 to 1.8 kg) mono, size 6 to 12 hooks, and a split shot for weight. Of course large trout and salmon require heavier tackle, but seldom will you need line heavier than 8-pound (3.6 kg) test or a hook larger than size 2.

The variety of trout and salmon baits is nearly endless. Garden worms, night crawlers, and salmon eggs are the most common baits, along with minnows and cut fish. Leeches, adult and larval insects, and crayfish are not as popular, but are no less effective. Fishermen have also discovered that certain "grocery baits," like marshmallows and corn, work extremely well, especially for stocked trout.

Although most trout will take any of these baits, some have a distinct preference. Also, a given bait may be more productive at certain times of year or under certain water conditions.

Fishermen have discovered that wax worms (bee moth larvae) and other larval baits used for ice fishing are excellent for trout. They work particularly well in winter, when most other baits are hard to find. Their small size is an advantage when the water is cold and trout feeding slows.

DRIFT FISHING

Drift fishing accounts for more trout and salmon than any other bait-fishing technique. The idea is to present your bait so it drifts naturally with the current, just like real food.

You can drift fish for everything from small brookies to trophy steelhead and salmon. The basic technique is the same, only the gear is different.

Position yourself to the side and just downstream of a riffle or run likely to hold trout. Most pools do not have enough current to keep your bait drifting. Before casting, look for boulders, logs, or other likely cover, then quarter your cast upstream so the bait will skirt the object as it drifts.

Light spinning gear works best for average-sized trout. A 6- to 7-foot (1.8 to 2.1 m) medium-action rod is long enough for good line control, yet flexible enough for lobbing delicate baits. The lighter the line you use, the easier it is to achieve a drag-free drift. Heavy line has more water resistance, so the current creates a larger belly and the bait begins to drift too fast. Limp, clear, 4-pound (1.8 kg) mono is a good all-around choice, but you may need heavier line if the bottom is snaggy.

Some drift fishermen use a fly rod with a spinning reel. The longer rod gives them even better line control and makes it easier to dunk the bait into hard-to-reach spots.

Steelhead and salmon anglers commonly use 8- to 10-weight fly rods, and fly reels loaded with 8- to 17-pound (3.6 to 7.7 kg) abrasion-resistant mono. With a rod this long, you can drift your bait, usually a spawn bag or some type of spawn imitation, through narrow runs with perfect control. Simply swing the bait upstream, walk it through the run, then swing it upstream again. This repetitious presentation is the best way to entice a strike from fish that aren't really feeding.

In drift fishing, it's important to select a sinker of the proper weight. Too heavy, and it will hang on the bottom so the bait cannot drift as fast as the current. Too light, and the current will lift the bait off the bottom. You must choose a sinker heavy enough so that it just ticks the bottom as the bait drifts. Carry a selection of sinkers and split shot in various sizes, and use different ones to suit the conditions.

Almost any natural bait tough enough to stay on the hook will work for drift fishing. A delicate bait like an adult mayfly would probably tear off. You can add visual appeal by snelling a small piece of fluorescent yarn on your hook just ahead of the bait. In fact, many steelhead and salmon anglers use only the yarn.

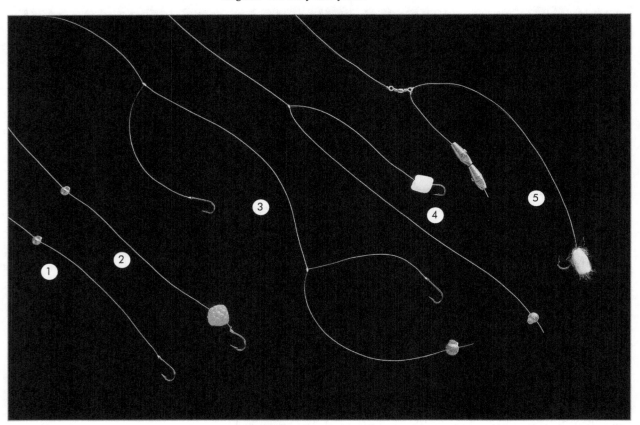

Drift-Fishing Rigs include: (1) Basic split shot rig; (2) Split shot rig with drift bobber for extra attraction and for keeping bait off bottom; (3) Double-dropper rig for fishing with two baits. The split shot pulls off when snagged; (4) Marshmallow rig for floating bait off bottom; and (5) Drift-sinker rig with yarn fly.

PLUNKING

Practically every experienced trout fisherman has been badly outfished at some time or other by a kid plunking worms into a pool. While the technique is not glamorous, it accounts for plenty of trout.

The term plunking simply means still-fishing. The usual technique is to attach a sinker to the line, bait up, lob a cast into a pool, then sit back and wait.

Plunking works especially well for big trout. If you sit quietly, they eventually detect the scent and swim over to investigate. If you continually cast and retrieve the bait, you are likely to spook them.

Almost any live bait will work, but night crawlers and minnows are most popular. In stocked streams, anglers often plunk with Velveeta cheese and other junk food. Browns, rainbows, and cutthroat seem most susceptible to plunking.

Use only enough weight to keep your bait from drifting. If you attach a heavy sinker, the fish will feel resistance and spit the bait. In small streams, a split shot is normally adequate, but in bigger streams, you may need a small slip sinker. Most anglers plunk with light spinning gear and 4- to 8-pound (1.8 to 3.6 kg) mono, depending on the size of the trout and the snagginess of the bottom.

PLUNKING TIPS

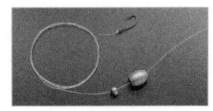

Make an easy-to-tie slip-sinker rig by threading an egg sinker onto the line, pinching on a small split shot about 2 feet (0.6 m) up the line, then attaching a hook.

Float your bait off the bottom by threading on a small marshmallow so it rides just ahead of the hook. Or, hook your bait on a floating jig head.

Chapter 6

TECHNIQUES FOR SPECIAL SITUATIONS

Woody Allen once said, "Eighty percent of success is just showing up." The same can be said of trout fishing. The reality is that not every day on the water is going to be perfect. Heavy rains, drought, heavy cover, darkness, and the long winter season, all can conspire to keep the fair-weather fisherman off the water. But the angler who knows how to handle these situations can extend his or her season and greatly increase their chances of success.

Of course, you should always check the regulations wherever you are planning to fish to ensure that it's legal to fish after dark, for example, or whether there is a winter trout-fishing season. In some states and provinces, prolonged drought can prompt fisheries managers to close rivers or regions to avoid excessive pressure on stressed fish, and high water can be particularly dangerous to the ill-prepared angler. But once you've determined the regulations, you can turn these special situations to your advantage.

The following pages will show you how to change up your approach, choose the proper gear, modify your casting style, or switch your fly and lure selection to adapt to whatever tricky conditions you may encounter. In fact, once you understand how to approach special situations, such as winter season or night fishing, you may find yourself reaching for your fishing gear when other fishermen are at home, giving you that most-cherished situation of all: a river to yourself.

HIGH WATER

To trout fishermen, high water can be a blessing or a curse. Runoff from a heavy rain or rapid snowmelt raises the stream level and discolors the water, but the effects of these changes depend upon the type of stream and your method of fishing.

Rising water draws anadromous trout and salmon into streams. Fishing may be tough as long as the water stays muddy, but as it starts to clear, the action picks up dramatically. Fishing peaks when the water is clearing, but still somewhat discolored.

Spin fishermen can get their lures deep simply by using more weight, but it's not as easy for fly fishermen. Split shot, lead-core line, shooting heads, and large weighted nymphs and streamers all help to solve the problem. However, trout still will have difficulty spotting a fly.

Flies and lures that produce vibration are more effective in discolored water. Trout detect the vibrations with their lateral-line sense. Bright colors also help. Fly materials like Flashabou, Krystal Flash, and tinsel improve the visibility of streamers and large wet flies. In extremely muddy water, natural bait—where allowed—can be most effective. Trout can smell the bait, even when they can't see it.

Streams vary in the amount of time necessary for the water to clear and return to normal level. It may take two weeks in a stream with a large drainage area, but only a few hours in one with a small drainage. In tailwater streams, the water may rise and fall daily.

Generally, headwaters clear first. If the lower reaches of a stream are too muddy for fly fishing, you may find water that's clear enough by moving upstream. Sometimes you only have to go far enough to get above a muddy tributary.

LOW WATER

When the water is low and the stream shrinks to a fraction of its former size, all the trout concentrate in a few key spots, usually the deepest pools, runs, and undercuts. Consequently, you can find the trout much more easily than in high water. But low water also means clear water, so the fish are spookier and more selective.

With the water so transparent, it's easier to walk along the stream and spot the trout, but they can also see you more clearly. The low water leaves them fewer places to hide, and thus more visible to predators, so the trout become much warier.

When trout become super-selective, fly fishermen gain an edge over anglers using other methods. Not only does a fly have a natural look, but it also allows a presentation more delicate than possible with other lures and baits. In low, clear water, fly fishermen use rods of 5-weight or lighter, leaders as long as 15 feet (4.6 m), and tippets as light as 7X.

Flies for low water are smaller than normal, usually size 16 or under, with drab, natural colors. Dries and nymphs generally work better than streamers. Terrestrial patterns, like a black ant, are a good choice when nothing is rising. Low-water periods usually correspond to the times when terrestrial insects are most numerous.

How you approach trout is even more important when the water is low and clear. Under these conditions, step lightly, keep a low profile, wear drab clothing and avoid throwing a shadow across the stream.

Low-water fishing is usually best in overcast or windy weather; trout cannot see you as well as they could under calm, sunny conditions. Trout are most active in early morning, around dusk, or at night. In midday, they tuck into heavy cover or move to deep water and feed very little.

HEAVY COVER

If you were to watch fisheries workers electrofishing a small trout stream, you'd be amazed at the number of trout living in dense brush piles, weed beds, and log jams, or far beneath undercut banks and overhanging limbs.

Stream trout are conditioned to seek heavy cover at an early age. Soon after they emerge from the redd, they face attacks from predatory insects, birds, and fish, including larger trout. Those that learn to find the cover that affords the greatest protection have the best chance of survival.

Many anglers do not even attempt to fish these prime spots, for fear of getting snagged. You can't escape the fact that snags will be a problem, but if you want to catch these wary trout, which usually are the biggest trout, you must learn to fish heavy cover.

By learning to side cast with a fly rod, for instance, you can place a fly beneath overhanging branches. A side cast is just like a conventional cast, except that you hold the rod parallel to the water. With a little practice you can cast beneath cover only a few inches off the water, precisely controlling your distance.

Fly fishing also works well for fishing undercut banks. You can often drift a fly beneath a bank that could not be reached with other lures or bait.

Trout tucked into dense weed beds are difficult to catch on spinning lures because weeds quickly foul the hooks. However, you can easily float a dry fly over the weed tops, or fish a sinking fly in pockets or channels in the weeds. With fly tackle you can cast across a weed bed to open water, retrieve the fly to the edge of the weeds, then pick it up for another cast without dragging it back through them.

Jigs work well for drawing trout out of heavy cover. Cast as close to a log jam, brush pile, or undercut as you can; a jig sinks fast enough to reach the fish zone before the current carries it away.

You can also draw trout from heavy cover with a spinner or small spoon. Position yourself upstream, cast down to the cover, then hang the lure in the current along the upstream edge and sides.

When you hook a trout, try to get it away from the cover immediately. If you let it run, it will invariably head for the thickest tangle of weeds or brush.

With any of these heavy-cover techniques, it pays to use heavier-than-normal line and tippets, preferably abrasion-resistant mono. Soft mono scuffs too easily and could cost you a good trout.

HOW TO FLY FISH AN UNDERCUT

Allow the fly to drift freely; if the current is angling into the bank, it will pull the fly beneath the overhang where trout can easily see it.

TIPS FOR FISHING HEAVY COVER

Flick a sidearm cast under overhanging brush. Raise the rod slightly on the back cast so the line won't slap the water behind you; lower it as the line unrolls to the rear, then make a forward cast just above the water.

Unsnag a fly by raising your rod tip, then throwing a loop as if making a roll cast. When the loop unrolls on the opposite side of the snag, the fly will usually pull free.

NIGHT FISHING

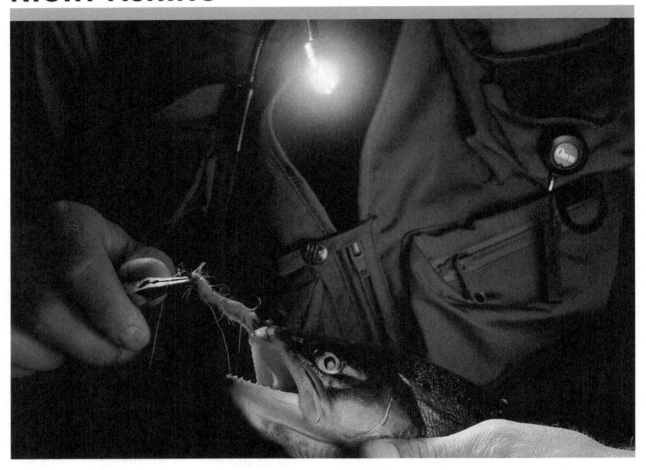

To many, the notion of fishing a trout stream at night evokes thoughts of tripping over logs and tangling lines in streamside brush. To others, night fishing means big trout, especially browns.

Big browns stay in heavy cover during daylight hours, but at night they seem to lose their caution. They feed in shallow riffles and tails of pools, often far from cover, and are not nearly as selective as in daylight. Cutthroat and rainbows also feed at night, but to a lesser extent.

Night fishing is most effective during low-water periods in summer, when the clarity increases because of the low flow, and the water temperature rises into the 70s (21°C). At night the water may cool to the mid-60s (17 to 18°C), a more likely temperature for feeding, and the clarity is actually an advantage. Moonless, starry nights are best; trout are less wary in the dark of the moon, but the stars provide enough light so you can see a little.

Before attempting to fish at night, scout the water during the day. Make note of likely trout lies, overhead branches, or other obstacles that could

Doctor plugs, spinners, and spoons with luminescent tape to improve lure visibility when night fishing. But do not use tape that glows too brightly; it will spook the fish. You can also buy luminescent fly-tying materials.

foul your cast, and deep holes that mean you could easily land a good-sized trout. Nighttime is not the time to check out new water.

Fly fishermen most commonly use streamers, nymphs, or leech imitations, usually in large sizes. During a major hatch, you can often hear trout rising. In this situation, dry flies can be very effective. Many night fishermen prefer big, heavily hackled dry flies because they are easier to see, and produce plenty of vibrations so trout can quickly locate them. A light-colored fly is also easier to see, and at night the exact color is not as important as the silhouette.

Because the fish are more aggressive at night, your presentation need not be as delicate as in daylight. In fact, a fly splatting down on the water may actually attract a trout's attention. You can get by with a 6- to 8-pound (2.7 to 3.6 kg) spinning line or fly tippet, so if you do get snagged in streamside brush you can pull loose.

You don't need a lot of special equipment for night fishing, but unless you're very familiar with the streambed, it's a good idea to wear waders instead of hip boots. Bug spray, a flashlight, and a light that attaches to your vest also come in handy.

TIPS FOR NIGHT FISHING

Attach your fly with a tiny metal clip. This way, you do not have to tie knots in the dark.

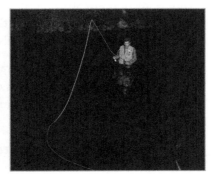

Spool on white fly line for night fishing. Any light-colored line will be visible, but white shows up best.

WINTER FISHING

If you dislike crowds, try fishing your favorite trout stream in winter. Chances are you'll have the whole stream to yourself, and the trout can be surprisingly cooperative.

Of course, you should check the fishing regulations to make sure the stream is open. Many streams close before the fall spawning season and don't reopen until spring, and those that remain open often have special regulations, such as artificials-only and catch-and-release.

Most winter fishing is for browns, rainbows, cutthroat, and brook trout, but anglers on Pacific coast streams catch good numbers of winter-run steelhead. These fish enter the streams in late fall in preparation for spring spawning.

Trout behave much differently in near-freezing water than at summertime temperatures. Look for them in slower water and heavier cover. In most cases they're right on the bottom, although they will rise to feed on tiny emerging midges, or snowflies. Bright sunlight triggers these midge hatches, prompting trout to start feeding. Fly fishing with midge pupa patterns in sizes 18 to 28 can be very effective, especially on warm, sunny afternoons.

Many anglers think that flies this small must be difficult to use, so they shy away from midge fishing. But you can fish midges much the same way you fish nymphs, only with lighter gear. Most midge fishermen use a 2- to 4-weight fly rod from 8 to 9 feet (2.4 to 2.7 m) long. Midges work best when fished just beneath the surface film, so a floating, weight-forward fly line is a good choice. Use a 9- to 12-foot (2.7 to 3.7 m) tapered leader with a 6X to 8X tippet. Strikes on midges are often very subtle, so it pays to attach a sensitive strike indicator.

Dry flies are seldom used in winter, but streamers, nymphs, and scud patterns account for a fair number of trout. Streamers should be worked deep and slow. Nymphs and scuds should be dead-drifted, just as in summer.

As a rule, the best winter trout fishing is where the stream is warmest. Trout often congregate around springs because the ground water is normally warmer than the surrounding water. In some tailwater streams, trout stay near the dam because water discharged from the depths of the upstream reservoir is a few degrees warmer than water farther downstream.

TIPS FOR FISHING A MIDGE

Check snowy stream banks to determine if there is a midge hatch. Tiny dark insects resembling mosquitoes are probably midges; select a fly that resembles them.

Dead drift a midge imitation just beneath the surface film, rather than on the surface. Your tippet will be less visible and the sunken fly seems to have more appeal.

Chapter 7

BLUE-RIBBON TROUT STREAMS

Finding a good place to fish has always been one of the biggest problems facing the average stream trout angler. In most regions of the country, prime trout water is at a premium, and local anglers are not always so generous when it comes to volunteering information on their favorite stream.

Over the last two decades, however, many trout-stream-rich states have devoted a great deal of time and money to producing publications and websites designed to help trout anglers find fishable waters. Many states now post signs along trout rivers detailing stream-access laws and fishing regulations. As the popularity of fly fishing soared during the early 1990s, many states realized the economic value of promoting trout-fishing-based tourism.

Guidebooks to trout water, once scarce and sketchy at best, are now readily available from a handful of publishers. Many of these books are updated regularly to keep abreast of changes in access and regulations.

Other good sources of information included detailed sporting atlases and map books, such as the DeLorme Gazetteers, which highlight trout-fishing hot spots with a trout symbol on rivers, streams, and lakes where trout can be found.

The following pages present an overview of the rivers and streams throughout the United States and Canada. This section is intended to help you locate trout and salmon waters in your home state and in regions where you may be traveling. Read on; you may be surprised to find trout in regions you never imagined they'd be found.

EASTERN STREAMS

Smith River, Virginia.

In North America, the sport of fly fishing for trout was born on eastern streams. Even today, streams like the Beaverkill are synonymous with quality fly fishing.

Despite extremely heavy fishing pressure, especially around population centers, eastern streams continue to provide good trout fishing. Many of the heavily fished streams must be stocked to meet the demand, but there are plenty of streams in remote areas with good populations of wild brook and brown trout. In fact, improving water quality in recent years has added to the number of trout-stream miles.

Most eastern trout streams are of the freestone variety. While these streams usually have good populations of trout, especially brookies, the fish sometimes run on the small side. Limestone streams are much less common but hold considerably larger trout, particularly browns. The better limestone streams typically produce numbers of 12- to 15-inchers (30.5 to 38.1 cm), with an occasional 4- to 6-pounder (1.8 to 2.7 kg). Fishing Creek, a limestone stream in Pennsylvania, produced a 15-pound, 4-ounce (6.8 kg, 113.4 g) brown trout in 1977.

Fly fishing on most eastern streams is best from April through June, the time of heaviest insect hatches.

The biggest eastern trout come from tailwater streams. Most are stocked with rainbows and browns, and commonly produce trophies from 8 to 10 pounds (3.6 to 4.5 kg). Although tailwater streams generally lack natural reproduction, they are quite fertile and have a long growing season because their water stays fairly warm during the winter. The warmer water also means that trout will start to bite earlier in the season than on most other streams. And in summer the water stays cool, so trout continue to bite.

The East's best fishing for brook trout is found in Maine, with some quality streams in Vermont and New Hampshire. If you want big brookies, 12- to 15-inchers (30.5 to 38.1 cm), look for a good-sized stream off the beaten track. The larger fish are quickly removed on heavily fished streams. Brook trout generally bite best from April through June on large streams, April through July on smaller ones.

Many lakes in the northern part of the region support populations of good-sized brook trout, brown trout, rainbow trout, and landlocked salmon. These species enter connecting streams in spring and fall for feeding and spawning, and offer excellent fishing opportunities. Spring fishing is best from April through June; fall fishing is best in September and October.

For those interested in quantity of trout more than size, mountain streams are the best bet. National forest lands throughout the East are laced with thousands of miles of small, out-of-the-way trout streams that produce plenty of 6- to 8-inch (15.2 to 20.3 cm) brookies. In the southern part of the region, mountain streams are the only ones cold enough to support trout. Fishing in most mountain streams starts picking up in March or April and stays good through the summer.

Eastern streams are not without their problems. Acid rain has affected trout fishing in some parts of the East, especially the Adirondacks. When streams acidify, brown trout are the first to disappear. Brook trout are more acid-tolerant and can persist longer, but even they have vanished from some streams.

Excessive fishing pressure has prompted special regulations on many eastern streams. Some streams have a no-kill regulation, meaning that all trout must be released. Others have trophy regulations, limiting anglers to one fish of specified trophy size. Other common regulations are fly fishing only or artificial lures only.

MIDWESTERN STREAMS

Trout Run Creek, Minnesota.

Most anglers picture a typical midwestern trout stream as a small, spring-fed creek flowing through a pasture. While hundreds of streams of this type are scattered throughout the Midwest, there are many other types of streams as well, including some of the country's finest trout water.

In the Dakotas, tailwater zones below Missouri River dams produce dozens of trophy browns and rainbows each season.

The Black Hills are laced with lightly fished trout streams that are very similar to quality streams in the West, but smaller in size. The main stems of these streams offer good fishing for browns and rainbows, the headwaters for brook trout.

Streams in the northern part of Michigan's lower peninsula grow much bigger brookies. In these larger, more fertile waters, the fish top out at about 17 inches (43.2 cm). In many of these streams, good-sized browns are found in the lower sections, where the water is warmer.

The streams of southeastern Minnesota, southwestern Wisconsin, and northeastern Iowa, in what's known as the Driftless Region, offer good fishing for a variety of trout. Many of these fertile streams flow through steep-sided limestone ravines and have ample supplies of spring water. Browns, the most common species, occasionally reach weights over 10 pounds (4.5 kg). Some of the streams are cold enough for brook trout, and a few support rainbows.

In the northern part of the region are numerous small, infertile streams flowing over beds of granite. These streams have very cold water and are best suited to brook trout. The fish are plentiful but grow very slowly, seldom exceeding 9 inches (22.9 cm).

The most famous midwestern streams, like Wisconsin's Brule and Michigan's Au Sable, are included in the section on Great Lakes tributaries.

Fishing in midwestern streams is usually best in spring and early summer, when streams are starting to warm, and in fall, when they start to cool. In summer, aquatic vegetation in streambeds sometimes makes fishing difficult. Heavy brush or tall weeds along the bank can also be a problem. In most streams, seasons close before the fall spawning period, but an increasing number reopen for a winter season, and a few remain open all winter.

Midwestern streams are plagued by a variety of problems ranging from overgrazing to flash flooding. When cattle are allowed to graze too close to the stream bank, they eat the vegetation that would keep the banks from eroding in high water. When the banks collapse, the streambed silts over, covering the gravel that produces insects and provides spawning habitat.

Flash flooding results mainly from excessive drainage of agricultural lands. With fewer lakes, ponds, and marshes to hold water, runoff flows directly into the streams, eroding the banks, creating massive log jams, and sometimes shifting portions of the channel.

Another common problem is beaver damage. Although beaver dams may create productive pools on high-gradient streams, they cause major problems on streams with lower gradients. They block spawning migrations, and the ponds that form above the dams have warm water and silty bottoms.

SOUTHERN STREAMS

Wilson Creek, North Carolina.

Trout fishing in the South doesn't get much press, but this region has a surprising number of good streams, including some that produce trout of world-record proportions.

Most southern streams, particularly those in the Deep South, are much too warm for trout. But streams with an ample supply of cold water from springs or cold-water draws often support healthy trout populations, as do streams at high altitudes, where the air is considerably cooler. Many of the best southern trout streams have a heavy overstory to shade the water and keep it cool.

Fluctuating water levels and siltation limit natural reproduction in most southern streams, so populations must be maintained by stocking.

The biggest trout come from tailwater streams, especially those where baitfish rather than insects are the primary forage. These large streams, fed by cold water from the depths of reservoirs, may stay cold enough for trout for 50 miles (80.5 km) or more below the dam.

Tailwater streams are stocked heavily with rainbows, but intense fishing pressure often crops them off before they reach trophy size. Nevertheless, the streams commonly produce 2- to 5-pound (0.9 to 2.3 kg) rainbows with an occasional 10- to 15-pounder (4.5 to 6.8 kg). Brown trout, being more difficult to catch, have greater trophy potential. Cutthroat trout have been stocked in some tailwater streams and are showing a lot of promise, with fish up to 9 pounds (4.1 kg) reported three years after stocking.

Fishing on most tailwater streams is best from late winter to midsummer. Downstream reaches of many tailwater streams become too warm for trout in late summer because not enough cold water is discharged from the dam.

Low- to medium-gradient limestone streams in Tennessee, the Kentucky Bluegrass region, and the Ozarks of Missouri and Arkansas also offer good trout fishing. Generally, these streams originate from large springs and flow through areas with a lot of exposed limestone rock.

A few of these streams support wild trout populations, but most are managed on a put-and-take or put-grow-and-take basis. Trout grow rapidly in the fertile water, but heavy fishing pressure removes most of them by the end of the season, before they have much chance to grow. Most run 10 to 14 inches (25.4 to 35.6 cm), with carry-over fish reaching 18 inches (45.7 cm).

Mountain streams in the Appalachians often have native brook trout, particularly in the headwaters. In many mountain streams, rainbows and browns have been stocked and are reproducing. Although these streams are fed by small springs, most are infertile, so trout grow slowly. Brook trout average only about 6 inches (15.2 cm), with a few reaching 12 inches (30.5 cm). Rainbows and browns run from 8 to 11 inches (20.3 to 27.9 cm), with a few up to 14 inches (35.6 cm).

The best mountain streams are those in state and national parks, some of which allow only catch-and-release fishing. Strip mining has degraded numerous mountain streams, and many Appalachian streams have been damaged by acid rain.

WESTERN STREAMS

Hat Creek, California.

The West is famed for its premier stream trout fishing, particularly in mountainous areas of Montana, Idaho, and Wyoming. Steelhead and salmon abound in the coastal streams of Washington and Oregon. This section in the book includes only the inland streams of the West. Here, the predominant species are rainbow, brown, and cutthroat trout; but many other salmonids are caught, including brook trout, bull trout, Dolly Varden, grayling, and golden trout.

Throughout the West, particularly in national forests and mountainous regions, there are thousands of miles of trout streams that seldom see a fisherman. This water is inaccessible by road, but you can find outstanding fishing if you do a little hiking. These streams have good populations of native trout and require no stocking.

Streams that are easy to reach are heavily fished, so they must be carefully regulated. On certain streams you must abide by slot limits; these require you to release trout within a specified size range. The Yellowstone River for a few miles below Yellowstone Lake is Wyoming's most popular trout stream, yet it produces an astounding number of 14- to 18-inch (35.6 to 45.7 cm) cutthroat because of a no-kill regulation.

In streams where cutthroat fishing is not strictly regulated, populations are quickly fished down. Cutthroat are easy to catch, and they do not compete well with other trout species.

Wading is the favorite way to fish most western streams, but some of the big rivers are too deep, and even if you could wade them, the best water is miles from the nearest road. So the only effective way to fish is by floating. McKenzie boats, specially designed for this type of fishing, are a common sight on the big rivers.

Western streams are known for good-sized trout, especially the famous rivers in southwestern Montana, like the Madison. These streams are cold yet fertile, so trout grow rapidly. Some have dozens of miles of prime trout water, and can absorb a lot of fishing pressure.

However, the biggest trout do not come from streams like the Madison, but from lakes and the rivers that feed and drain them. Tailwater streams, like the South Fork of the Snake River below Idaho's Palisades Reservoir, yield a surprising number of trophy trout, including browns over 15 pounds (6.8 kg).

Most western streams are fed by snowmelt from the mountains. You can catch some trout in early spring, but once the heavy snowmelt begins, fishing is tough. It picks up again after the streams subside. The best fishing is often in fall, when streams are low and stable, and fishermen become more interested in hunting.

Tailwater streams warm more slowly than those fed by surface runoff. Insect hatches and peak fishing times run about a month later.

The salmon fly hatch is an important event on the calendar of western anglers, especially those in the vicinity of Yellowstone Park. During the hatch, usually in late June or early July, trout gorge themselves on the emerging nymphs and fishermen enjoy some of the year's fastest action.

Although the West abounds with quality trout water, many streams face serious problems. De-watering for irrigation and domestic use sometimes reduces flow to the point where a stream actually dries up. Another common problem is erosion, caused by overgrazing of stream banks.

CANADIAN STREAMS

Kazan River, Northwest Territories.

Canadian streams seldom receive the acclaim given to prime trout waters in the United States. Nonetheless, some Canadian streams offer trout fishing unmatched anywhere else in North America.

Because the climate is so cold, streams that would be too warm for trout if located farther south stay cold enough through the summer. Despite the climate, Canadian streams produce lots of good-sized trout. Many of the streams are large and fertile, a good combination for growing big fish. Another contributing factor is the light fishing pressure.

Streams of the Atlantic provinces and the Hudson Bay drainage support some of the world's largest brook trout, with fish in the 6- to 8-pound (2.7 to 3.6 kg) class caught each year. The biggest brookies come from streams that draw sea-run fish or those that are connected to inland lakes. Fishing is best in the Atlantic provinces from mid-June to late July, and in Hudson Bay tributaries from early August to mid-September.

The Atlantic provinces also boast world-class fly fishing for Atlantic salmon. The fish run about 8 to 12 pounds (3.6 to 5.5 kg) and top out around 40 pounds (18.2 kg). Peak fishing time is mid-June to late July. Access is carefully controlled on the best salmon rivers, and you may have to pay a daily fee to fish them.

Arctic char, one of the hardest-fighting freshwater fish, can be caught along Canada's northern coast, especially from the Coronation Gulf east. In the better rivers, char run 12 to 14 pounds (5.5 to 6.4 kg), with the potential for a 30-pounder (13.6 kg). Most char rivers are north of the tree line, so they stay ice-free for only about two months, July and August.

Grayling are common in the northern half of Canada, from Hudson Bay west. Some of the better grayling streams are those of the Mackenzie River drainage, and those along the tree line from Great Bear Lake to Churchill, Manitoba. Grayling typically run from 1 to 2 pounds (0.45 to 0.9 kg), but the prime streams produce numbers of 2½- to 3-pounders (1.1 to 1.4 kg), with an occasional fish up to 5 pounds (2.3 kg). Grayling fishing is best just after ice-out because the fish are concentrated in spawning areas. Fishing stays good all summer, unless the fish move back to a larger river or lake when spawning has been completed.

Streams in the mountainous region of western Canada offer the greatest variety of trout species. You'll find excellent summertime rainbow fishing in the Central Interior Plateau region of British Columbia, east of the coastal mountains. Most of the fish run 1 to 3 pounds (0.45 to 1.4 kg), but 5- to 8-pounders (2.3 to 3.6 kg) aren't unusual. Brown trout of similar size abound on the east slope of the Rockies in central Alberta. June and October are the best months, but fishing is good all summer. In the eastern Kootenay Mountains of southeastern British Columbia, cutthroat run exceptionally large, with a number of 3- to 5-pounders (1.4 to 2.3 kg) caught each year, mainly from late July through August. Rivers in the Kootenays also produce trophy-class bull trout, with occasional fish up to 25 pounds (11.4 kg).

Even though angling pressure is light in most regions of Canada, overfishing is a common problem on easily accessible streams. The short growing season limits trout production, so strict regulations are often needed to control the harvest. The very best fishing areas are accessible only by air.

GREAT LAKES TRIBUTARIES

Betsie River, Michigan.

Tributaries flowing into the Great Lakes draw heavy runs of lake-dwelling trout and salmon. Some of these streams rival the famous coastal streams of the Pacific Northwest in the number and size of salmonids they draw. Many tributaries also support good populations of resident trout.

A wide variety of streams flow into the Great Lakes, ranging from tiny creeks that completely stop flowing in dry periods, to silty, warm water rivers large enough for seagoing vessels. Many of these streams do not fit into the usual stream categories, so classifications are not shown on the maps.

The best trout and salmon streams are spring-fed and have a relatively consistent flow; here, the fish reproduce naturally. In areas with good trout and salmon populations, almost all tributaries draw some spawners, though reproduction may not be successful.

Great Lakes tributaries are best known for their outstanding steelhead fishing. While the steelhead do not grow quite as large as those in coastal streams, 15-pounders (6.8 kg) are not unusual and 20- to 25-pounders (9.1 to 11.4 kg) are taken occasionally. The largest steelhead come from tributaries of Lake Ontario and from Canadian tributaries of Lake Huron.

Steelhead run in spring and again in fall. They spawn during the spring run; the fall run is a false run, meaning that no spawning takes place. Skamania steelhead, a summer-run strain that commonly reaches weights over 15 pounds (6.8 kg), have been stocked in some Great Lakes tributaries.

The exact timing of the spring run depends on water temperature and stream flow. As a rule, the water must rise to 40°F (4.4°C) before steelhead will start to enter the stream. Then, a heavy rain that causes stream levels to rise will draw large numbers of steelhead from the lake. Rain is also needed to trigger the fall run.

Besides steelhead, Great Lakes tributaries get good fall runs of coho, chinook, and pink salmon. Some streams have good fall runs of brook or brown trout, and a few even draw lake trout.

On some tributaries, the summer or winter flow drops so low that a sandbar forms at the mouth. Fish cannot enter the stream until heavy runoff washes out the sandbar.

Many Great Lakes tributaries have some type of barrier, like a dam or waterfall, a short distance from the mouth. The barrier blocks the upstream movement of migratory salmonids. Only resident trout are found above it. Be sure you know the location of the barrier because fishing regulations above may differ from those below. Sometimes, natural resources agencies install fish ladders or build step pools to allow migratory salmonids to reach upstream spawning areas.

COASTAL STREAMS

Nushagak River, Alaska.

Famed for their unparalleled Pacific salmon and steelhead fishing, the coastal streams of Oregon, Washington, British Columbia, and Alaska attract anglers from across the continent. In addition to salmon and steelhead, many of these streams draw good runs of sea-run Dolly Varden and cutthroat trout. Numerous streams in Alaska and northern British Columbia also have excellent populations of resident rainbows and Arctic grayling.

The anadromous species get most of the attention because of their considerably larger size. Steelhead commonly run up to 20 pounds (9.1 kg), with record fish weighing in at over 40 pounds (18.2 kg). Chinook salmon frequently grow to 50 pounds (22.7 kg); record fish approaching 100 pounds (45.5 kg) have been taken in the Kenai River, Alaska.

The timing of salmon runs varies considerably with latitude. The chinook run in Alaska starts about two months earlier than the run in Oregon. But the sequence of spawning runs of different species remains the same. Steelhead move into the streams in early spring, followed in order by chinooks, sockeyes, pinks, and chums, then cohos and fall-run steelhead.

Alaska runs are shorter in duration than those farther south because of the colder climate. Thus, the fish are more concentrated, resulting in excellent fishing. The best streams for variety, size, and numbers of fish are found in southwest Alaska.

Runs of the same species take place at different times in different streams. Runs begin earlier in streams where the fish have to swim great distances to reach their spawning grounds.

Summer-run steelhead, for instance, may enter a stream in July, then swim hundreds of miles upstream before spawning the following March. Winter-run steelhead may move into a shorter stream in February, running upstream only a fraction of the distance before spawning a month later. A few streams have both summer- and winter-run fish.

Rainfall and tides have a great influence on steelhead and salmon runs. Increased flow from a heavy rain draws the fish into the stream. Fishing is best when the water starts to clear. The fish also ride in on high tides.

In some rivers, trout and salmon swim hundreds of miles upstream to reach their spawning grounds; the very best fishing, especially in Alaska and British Columbia, is in areas accessible only by float plane or a long boat ride.

Coastal streams are fed mainly by surface runoff and are relatively infertile. For most anadromous species, though, fertility of the stream is not important; the adults enter streams to spawn, and they feed very little during the migration.

On many coastal streams, dams have blocked migration routes, so trout and salmon cannot reach their spawning grounds. To maintain salmonid populations, natural resources agencies must stock these streams.

Dams also create another problem; the plunging water becomes supersaturated with nitrogen. The blood of fish below the dam absorbs too much nitrogen, causing gas-bubble disease, which may be fatal. This problem has been corrected on most streams by redesigning the dams to eliminate plunging water. Other threats to salmonid populations include commercial fishing and Indian netting.

Fishing for resident rainbows peaks in fall; grayling are easily caught throughout the season. Practically all resident trout follow the spawning salmon, feeding heavily on their eggs. After the salmon leave, the resident fish disperse, becoming more difficult to find.

The sportfishing season on most coastal streams is continuous, although some streams or sections of them are closed for a time in ensure that enough fish reach the spawning grounds to produce a satisfactory year-class.

A FEW WORDS ON CONSERVATION

Not long ago, while in a remote area of British Columbia, I had the opportunity to fish for the rare and beautiful bull trout (*Salvelinus confluentus*) in one of the last places on earth where these char still survive—and where it was still legal to catch and release them. After a long dusty drive on a bone-jarring logging road, and an equally challenging climb down an unmarked trail, the dense forest opened to reveal a clear emerald-tinted pool filled with enormous and brightly colored bull trout resting for their last push to the spawning grounds upstream.

The first fish I hooked exceeded the 26 inches (66 cm) the Canadian government said was the maximum size for this species. The next fish shattered my 6-weight fly rod. The last fish, caught on a back-up 7-weight rod, measured a remarkable 31 inches (78.7 cm) and was roughly two feet (0.61 m) around.

As I held the fish briefly for a photograph, it was difficult to imagine that there was once a bounty on this species, and that without protection (including from anglers like me) they might disappear altogether in my lifetime.

Only a century and a half ago, the Atlantic salmon (*Salmo salar*) and Pacific salmon (*Oncorhynchus spp*) were so plentiful that coastal rivers throughout the Northern Hemisphere ran with seemingly inexhaustible populations. Today, at least 106 species of Pacific salmon are extinct, and the Atlantic salmon continues to fight for survival despite a moratorium on commercial fishing in many parts of the North Atlantic.

In Yellowstone Lake, in Yellowstone National Park, the native cutthroat (*Oncorhynchus clarki bouvieri*) were a prized (if easily caught) species. But in the mid-1990s non-native and predatory lake trout (*Salvelinus namaycush*) were discovered in the lake, reportedly stocked illegally by "bucket biologists" a decade earlier. Today, despite efforts to eradicate the lake trout, the entire population of native Yellowstone cutthroat trout is threatened with extinction.

In each of the above cases—and countless others like them—fish that were once plentiful are now being pushed to the brink of extinction.

The legendary fly fisherman, Lee Wulff, once said, "A good gamefish is too valuable to be caught only once." The author John Gierach wrote that "trout are so incongruously pretty as to seem otherworldly," and that they are "among those creatures who are ... a lot prettier than they need to be." And so they are. Yet they are at risk of disappearing if we don't learn to protect the places where they live, and the sources of the cold water that feed their native streams.

Trout and salmon conservation goes beyond catch-and-release. It involves tackling complex and controversial issues such as habitat improvement, special fishing regulations, dam removal, fish-stocking policies, grazing and agricultural practices, and even stream access laws. Conservation organizations, such as Trout Unlimited, work to bring diverse interests, such as industry, government, sportfishing groups, and the general public together to find a way to preserve the natural resources while meeting the needs of all. It's no easy task. But each angler can make a difference.

INDEX

A

Accessories, 59–63
Air temperatures, 43
Appalachian mountain streams, 129
Arctic char
  about, 13
  finding blue-ribbon, 133
  spawning season, 27
Arctic grayling
  about, 13
  spawning season, 27
Atlantic salmon
  about, 12
  spawning season, 27

B

Bait, natural, 107–108, 110
Baitfish, 76
Blood knots, 78
Breathable waders, 62
Brook trout
  about, 13
  appearance of, 9
  spawning season, 27
Brown trout
  about, 11
  spawning season, 27
Bucktails, 92
Bull trout
  about, 13
  spawning season, 27

C

Caddisflies
  about, 21
  imitation, 85
Canada, trophy fishing in, 132–133
Casting
  in fly fishing
    basic overhead, 80
    common mistakes, 83
    double hauls, 82
    false, 81
    overview of, 79–80
    shooting line, 82
    using reach cast, 86
    using roll cast, 83
    using S-cast, 86
  with hardware, 100–102

Catch-and-release fishing
  natural bait and, 107–108
  techniques, 71
  trout yields and, 70
Chars
  Arctic
    about, 13
    in Canada, 133
    finding blue-ribbon, 133
    spawning season, 27
  stream dwelling, 13
  See also Trout
Chinook salmon
  about, 14
  spawning season, 27
Chum salmon
  about, 14
  spawning season, 27
Clippers, 59
Clothing
  fingerless gloves, 60
  rain jackets, 61
  stream cleats, 63
  vests, 61–62
  waders and hip boots, 62–63
  wading belts, 63
Cloud cover, 43
Coastal cutthroat trout, 12
Coastal rainbow trout, 11
Coho salmon
  about, 14
  spawning season, 27
Conservation, 138–139
Crayfish flies, 95
Creel, 59
Cross-stream retrieve, 99
Cutthroat trout
  about coastal, 12
  about West Slope, 12
  about Yellowstone, 11
  spawning season, 27

D

Diet
  common foods, 19, 20–22
  imitating with flies, 75
  overview of, 18
Dissolved oxygen in water, 33
Dog salmon, 14

Dolly Varden
  about, 13
  appearance of, 9
  spawning season, 27
Double clinch knots, 78
Double hauls, 82
Downstream fishing
  drifting (baitcasting), 99
  fly fishing with S-cast, 86
  with S-cast, 88
  trolling, 104
Drift fishing, 109–111
Drifting (baitcasting), 99
Dropper rigs, 106
Drying agents, 61
Duncan loop knots, 78

E

Eastern states
  checking regulations in, 125
  freestone streams in, 124
  limestone streams in, 124
  overfishing in, 139
  tailwater streams in, 125
  trophy fishing in, 124–125
Eggs, 26
Eyeglasses, 61

F

Fingerless gloves, 60
Fishing accessories
  clippers, 59
  creel, 59
  fingerless gloves, 60
  floatants, 60
  fly box, 60
  forceps, 60
  gravel guards, 63
  hook hones, 60
  illustration, 59
  insect nets, 60
  insect repellent, 60
  landing nets, 60
  leader sinks, 60
  leader straighteners, 60
  leader wallets, 60
  leader wraps, 60
  line cleaners, 60
  needle-nose pliers, 61
  notebooks, 61

polarized glasses, 61
priests, 61
rain jackets, 61
retractor reels, 61
silicone powder, 61
split shot, 61
stomach pumps, 61
stream cleats, 63
Swiss army knives, 61
tape measures, 61
tippet material, 61
vest lights, 62
vests, 61–62
waders and hip boots, 62–63
wader staffs, 62
wading belts, 63
water thermometers, 62
Flies
  fly fishing with
    dry, 84–86, 121
    special purpose, 94–95
    wet, 87–88
  hooking, playing, and landing
  trout on, 68
  imitating insects with, 75
  spinning and baitcasting with,
  105–106
Floatants, 60
Floating lines, 52
Floating/sinking lines, 52–53
Fly boxes, 60
Fly fishing
  casting
    basic overhead, 80
    common mistakes, 83
    double hauls, 82
    false, 81
    overview of, 79–80
    shooting line, 82
    using reach cast, 86
    using roll cast, 83
    using S-cast, 86
  with dry flies, 84–86
  in high water, 114
  leaders, 54–56
  lines, 50–53
  in low water, 114
  at night, 118–119
  with nymphs, 89–91
  rigging up, 77–78
  rods and reels, 47–49
  with special purpose flies, 94–95

in spring, 7
with streamers, 92–93
in water with heavy cover, 116–117
with wet flies, 87–88
Fly leaders, 54–56
Fly lines, 50–53
Fly rods, 46–48
Forceps, 60
Freestone streams
  in east, 124
  fertility of, 29
  gradients and characteristics of, 36

G
Gierach, John, 139
Gloves, fingerless, 60
Golden trout
  about, 12
  spawning season, 27
Grasshopper patterns, 95
Gravel guards, 63
Graylings, stream dwelling, 13
Great Lakes, trophy fishing in,
  134–135
Growth rate, 18–19

H
Habitat
  channel shape, 30–31
  dissolved oxygen in, 33
  diversity, 30–31
  pH level, 33
  preferences, 33
  shade, 32
  stability of flow, 32
  typical, 34–37
  water bottom type, 30–31
  water clarity, 32
  water fertility, 29
  water gradients, 30
  water temperatures, 30, 32
Hardware, described, 100
Hardware fishing, 100–102
Hatch charts for insects, 22
Hatchery vs. wild trout, 28
Head-and-tail rises, 24
High water fishing, 114
Hip boots, 62–63
Homing, 27

Hook hones, 60
Hooking, playing, and landing,
  67–69
Hooks, 77–78
Humpback salmon, 14
Hydraulics of streams, 39

I
Insect nets, 60
Insect repellent, 60
Insects
  common stream, 20–22
  hatch charts for, 22
  imitating with flies, 75
  rises and, 23–24

J
Jackets, 61
Jig fishing, 98–99
Juvenile stages, 26

K
King salmon, 14
Knots, 78

L
Landing nets, 60
Larval baits, 108
Later line, 17
Leader sinks, 60
Leader straighteners, 60
Leader wallets, 60
Leader wraps, 60
Leech flies, 95
Life span, 19
Limestone streams
  in east, 124
  fertility of, 29
  gradients and characteristics of, 37
  in south, 129
Line cleaners, 60
Lines
  for fly fishing, 52–53
  monofilament, 97
  shooting in fly fishing, 82
  for spinning and baitcasting, 58
Loops, tying, 77

M

Mayflies
  about, 20
  imitation, 84–85
Midges
  about, 22
  imitation, 85
  winter fishing and, 121
Midwestern states
  tailwater streams in, 126
  trophy fishing in, 126–127
Monofilament lines, 97
Muddlers, 92, 93

N

Natural bait, 107–108, 110
Needle-nose pliers, 61
Neoprene waders, 62
Nets, 60
Netting, 69
Night fishing, 118–119
Notebooks, 61
Nymphs, fly fishing with, 89–91,
  121

O

Overhead casting, 80

P

Pacific salmon, 14
pH level of water, 33
Pink salmon
  about, 14
  spawning season, 27
Playing, 68
Pliers, needle-nose, 61
Plunking, 111
Polarized glasses, 61
Pools, 39
Priests, 61
Pumps, 61

R

Rain, 42–43
Rainbow trout
  about, 11
  spawning season, 11
Rain jackets, 61
Reach cast, 86
Red salmon, 14
Reels
  for fly fishing, 48–49
  for spinning and baitcasting, 58
Reel seats, 48
Regulations, checking
  in east, 125
  generally, 113
  for Great Lakes tributaries, 135
  in west, 131
Releasing fish, 71
Retractor reels, 61
Riffles, 39
Rigging up, 77–78
Rises, 23–24
Rod action, 47–48
Rods
  for fly fishing, 47–48
  for spinning and baitcasting, 57–58
Roll cast, 83
Runs, 39

S

Salmon
  characteristics of, 7, 10
  growth rate of, 19
  overview of, 9–10
  Pacific dwelling, 14
  stream dwelling, 12
  types of, 12, 14
Salmon eggs, imitating, 95
Salmonidae family, 9
Salmon runs, 136–137
S-cast, 86, 88
Scud patterns, 95, 121
Seasons
  spawning, 11, 27
  spring fishing, 7
  winter fishing, 120–121
Senses
  smell, 16–17, 108
  vibrations, 17
  vision, 15–16
Shooting heads/shooting tapers, 52
Side planers, 103
Silicone powder, 61
Silver salmon, 14
Sinking lines, 52
Sink tip lines, 52–53
Sip rises, 24
Sites for spawning, 25
Slipping, 104
Smell, sense of, 16–17, 108
Sockeye salmon
  about, 14
  spawning season, 27
Southern states
  tailwater streams in, 128–129
  trophy fishing in, 128–129
Spawning behavior, 25–27
Speckled trout
  about, 13
  appearance of, 9
Spinning and baitcasting
  with flies, 105–106
  in high water, 114
  monofilament lines for, 97
  in spring, 7
  tackle for, 57–58
  techniques
    casting with hardware, 100–102
    drift fishing, 109–110
    jig fishing, 98–99
    plunking, 111
    trolling, 103–104
  in water with heavy cover, 116–117
Splashes, 24
Split shot, 61
Spooking, tips to minimize, 65
Spring creeks, 37
Spring fishing, 7
Staffs for wading, 62
Steelhead runs, 135, 137
Steelhead trout, 11
Still-fishing, 111
Stomach pumps, 61
Stoneflies
  about, 21
  imitation, 85
Stream cleats, 63
Stream dwelling fish
  chars, 13
  graylings, 13
  salmon, 12
  types of, 11–14
Streamers, fly fishing with, 92–93,
  121
Streams
  common insects in, 20–22
  finding blue-ribbon
  Canadian, 131–133
  coastal, 136–147
  eastern, 124–125
  Great Lakes tributaries, 134–135
  midwestern, 126–127
  overview of, 123
  southern, 128–129
  western, 130–131

fishing in high water, 114
fishing in low water, 115, 118
fishing in water with heavy cover, 116–117
fly fishing across, 86
recognizing improvement devices in, 40, 41
stability of flow, 32
   See also Water
Swiss army knives, 61

T

Tailing, 24
Tailwater streams
   about, 37
   in east, 125
   in midwest, 126
   in south, 128–129
   in west, 131
Tape measures, 61
Techniques, 111
Terrestrials, 94–95
Thermometers, 62
Tippet material, 61
Tippet size chart, 56
Trolling, 103–104
Trophy trout, fishing for
   in Canadian streams, 132–133
   in eastern streams, 124–125
   finding and techniques, 72–73
   in midwestern streams, 126–127
   in southern streams, 128–129
   with streamers, 92–93
   in western streams, 130–131

Trout
   characteristics of, 7, 10, 28
   growth rate of, 19
   hatchery v. wild, 28
   overview of, 9–10
   types of stream dwelling, 11–12

U

Undercuts, fishing, 117
Upstream
   fishing a nymph, 91
   trolling, 104

V

Vertical jigging, 99
Vest lights, 62
Vests, 61–62
Vibrations, 17
Vision, 15–16

W

Waders, 62–63
Wader staffs, 62
Wading
   techniques for, 66
   in western streams, 131
Wading belts, 63
Water
   bottom type, 30–31
   clarity, 32
   dissolved oxygen in, 33
   fertility, 29
   gradients, 30
   pH level, 33

   reading, 40–41
   recognizing improvement devices in, 40, 41
   stability of flow, 32
   temperature
      about, 30
      cold, 32
      at night, 118
      preferences, 9
      in winter, 120, 121
   terms for parts of stream, 39
   understanding moving, 38–39
   See also Streams
Water fertility, 29
Water thermometers, 62
Weather, 42–43
Western states
   checking regulations in, 131
   overfishing in, 139
   tailwater streams in, 131
   trophy fishing in, 130–131
West Slope cutthroat trout, 12
Wet-fly drifts, 88
Wet-fly drift technique, 88, 93
Windy weather, 43
Winter fishing, 120–121
Wulff, Lee, 139

Y

Yellowstone cutthroat trout, 11

Z

Zonkers, 92

CPSIA information can be obtained at www.ICGtesting.com
Printed in the USA
LVOW02s0643190814

399546LV00011B/12/P

9 781591 866312